Acclaim for Cathy Arellano's

Salvation on Mission Street

Cathy Arellano walks a sure foot from narrative poem to performative story to lyric fiction in this first collection, the seedling for new Mission Literature. Highly recommended for young and old alike; seasoned poets or literate laborers will *aprovechar* this book — con gusto. Buy *Salvation* for salvation, then pass it around.

Lorna Dee Cervantes, author of *Emplumada*

This compilation of sweet short stories and poems about family, love and loss in San Francisco's Mission District made me smile, laugh, and feel the pain of heartbreak. Each page brought to life the Martinez family's everyday life, celebrations, and losses during a special pocket of time for a community that is currently going through its own losses. Having grown up in the Mission District, I felt a sense of pride revisiting the colorful places, events, and traditions that we experienced as youth, as well as the racism, police brutality, and homophobia that has always plagued the community and compromised the lives of Latinos. I felt connected to Barril with her love, fears, sadness and a sense of injustice. As a young queer Latina who often seems like the odd girl out, she tries to figure out her place in this family, amongst her group of friends and in this community. She quietly observes and admires from afar as she tries to fit in. She doesn't always succeed in fitting in but does come out stronger and wiser with each experience.

Karla Castillo, Counselor, San Francisco State University
(former Program Manager, Mission Girls Services for Latinas)

I attended several readings in Albuquerque where Cathy Arellano was one of the featured readers, and her street-smart style and delivery never failed to convey the love and respect she has for familia, the neighborhood, and her people. She is a Chicana storyteller par excellence, and her writing is packed with minute detail, rich imagery, and laced with the warmth and wit of the barrio. And she knows her history, too. Not the crap they teach in the public schools, but the history they don't want us to know. Sit up and take notice as she speaks out against the gentrification (another term for "modern colonization") of her beloved Mission neighborhood. Cathy Arellano's first collection of prose and poetry is a welcome addition to our culture's literary canon.

Richard Vargas, author of *Guernica, Revisited,* and Editor/Publisher of *The Más Tequila Review*

Cathy Arellano's narrative of the Mission past and present provides the reader a visual inside to a changing community from long gone "familiar times" to the current days of constant upheaval produced by shifting community through gentrification. Her story is one of a colorful and vibrant community, of people's lives, and constant change. Arellano shares a tightly woven narrative that makes you feel the warmth of the sun for which this neighborhood is known. You don't need to have grown up in the Mission to understand the stories of our youth. Wherever your community, childhood memories will flush to the forefront as you read her stories because they are universal and commonplace. You will recognize your voice in hers in the accounts about family, relations, crushes, death, and change. As a reader who grew up in the same neighborhood as Arellano, I am taken back to the Mission, to experience the emotional recollections of old storefronts and hangouts.

Kathryn Blackmer-Reyes, Librarian, San José State University

Salvation
on Mission Street

Salvation
on Mission Street

Cathy Arellano
foreword by Cherríe L. Moraga

Kórima Press

Earlier versions of the following poems first appeared in the publications noted below:

"Mission Walls" first appeared in Malpaís Review, Volume 2 Issue 4, 2012.

"Free the Mission" and "Free Ramona" first appeared in Huizache, Issue 2, 2012.

"Casanova" first appeared in Sinister Wisdom: A Multicultural Lesbian Literary Arts & Art Journal, Issue 74, 2008.

"Out With the Family" first appeared in Days I Moved Through Ordinary Sounds: The Teachers of WritersCorps in Poetry and Prose, 2009.

"Dot Com Boom" first appeared in Label Me Latino, 2012.

"Salvation on Mission Street" first appeared in Tongues Magazine, 2002.

"Gentrification Is When" first appeared in Malpaís Review, Volume 2 Issue 4, 2012.

"If You Can't on Mission Street" first appeared in El Tecolote, 2010 and Feminist Formations, Volume 25 Issue 1, Spring 2013.

"Martinez Family Map" first appeared in Feminist Formations, Volume 25 Issue 1, Spring 2013.

Cover Art Title: Harvest
Artist: Amaryllis DeJesus Moleski
Medium: Spray paint on adobe wall
Location: Peñasco, New Mexico
Year: 2011
Artist Website: www.amaryllisdejesusmoleski.com
Instagram: @wildhomegirl

Author photograph by Rebeka Rodriguez

Book Design: Lorenzo Herrera y Lozano

Published by Kórima Press
San Francisco, CA
www.korimapress.com

ISBN: 978-0692692455

for

Uncle Joe
Uncle John
Grandpa
Mom
Hillary
Uncle Tony
Mary
Cece
Nana
Eric
Horacio

Contents

Foreword

Salvation on Mission Street may not save lives, but it offers a map of memory that might very well save the *soul* of the place.

In this collection of poems and home-grown stories, Cathy Arellano introduces us to a pueblo—a vanishing tribe of pre-gentrification San Francisco Mission District Raza—living close to extinction, resultant of the turn-of-the century invasion of hipster culture and dot-commer incomes. In these pages, Arellano sings a bitter sweet song of nostalgia and deep love for an almost erased neighborhood and the poet's matrilineal family that resided in it. Her litany of bars and ice cream shops and parks and street corners and curbsides and social clubs becomes its own extended protest poem against the daily erasure of a culture of Mexican, Central American and Native city dwellers who once (and still) work in nearby factories, panaderías, and government buildings; who spread out blankets on the floor of their rented flats each night to accommodate the extra live-in relatives.

What is deprivation to some is 'home' to others. This book reminded me of this, of the uncalculated price tag of economic privilege: the loss of the intimate proximity of relations; the regañadas (scoldings) by aunts and uncles, where nicknames of ridicule—"tonta" (stupid) and "burra" (donkey)—are understood as "I love you;" the way a Lawrence Welk rendition of "roll out the barrel" somehow anoints a chubby schoolgirl as an honored member of her familia.

Salvation paints an urban mural of language, where the clashes and contradictions between race and gender and sexuality and class entitlement all rub up against one another, igniting an emergent política inside the poet-daughter-first-generation-college-goer-chicana-lesbian imagination. Her young world is lettered by the acronyms of the times. No hashtags, but the bold life-sized "FMLN" letters of a living 1980s revolution three thousand miles south and of free "Los Siete" meetings just down the street, a decade before. As young scribe, Arellano silently takes note through image in word.

"She tossed my wrinkled Pendleton at me like we meant nothing to her. " This may be my favorite lesbian line in the book, describing the brutal stab of middle school homophobic indifference from the "finest chola in ALL of San Pancho." Because it's just so damn true and ordinary and *poetically* unjust. So much of this reading invites the humbling nod of recognition. *I been there*, the reader will confer. And, for my part, I am grateful for the reminder.

There is one word, however, *not* written in these pages, but is read wordlessly in every verse and in every cuento: *neo-colonization*. Arellano does not use the word here, because it is not a word for the heart. It is not the word to speak of that intimate quality of Chicana lesbian desire that somehow (at least in *this* reader's mind) connects the loss of a Motown-loving painted-lipped high femme mother with the loss of a Mexican barrio. "I won't be fine. I need her (it)," the poet implores upon her mother's (and neighborhood's) passing. It is a queer connection, to be sure, as Arellano land-marks the unfolding Mission history inscribed here with every eviction and inner-city move required of her extended familia ("Map").

Partly in protest, partly in lament, *Salvation on Mission Street* asserts in its final pages: We were here first. Remember? "Thirty-Eight Oh Two/two bedrooms, two half bathrooms/so many mouths to feed/ we ate in shifts." Remember? A history that "swims back 235 years/ when the ohlone and miwok walked freely/on their land/now their graves." And we are still around, Cathy Arellano insists, as she "whittle[s] all [her] wars to [this] one battle" cry to save the soul of the Mission.

Cherríe L. Moraga
Oakland, Califas

Introduction

"Let me take your picture," Mom pointed her Vivitar 110 at me.

"Aw, Mom." My eyes were still spider-webbed with mascara.

"You left before I could even take a picture."

"Mom," I whined.

"Just one."

I showed some teeth, did one of those not-quite-smiling smiles.

"It was a special day for me too, mija."

Click.

The manila-colored parchment paper with old English letters rests in my right hand, the gold, satiny finish in my left. My thick, long hair is pinned back with a large barrette. I'm wearing my army green Clash t-shirt and 501s. I tore the sky blue dress when I came home from the Senior Boat Dance very early that morning. She had taken me shopping at Macy's for that and my prom dress—a white, layered chiffon, asymmetrical number. Her and my sister had helped me apply—no, she applied without interference from me—the mascara, some blush and lipstick. I never again wore the grey, patent leather heels with a bow over the toes or either of those dresses. Mom took one of her vacation days to stay home with me and clean up after the party from the night before.

It was a special day for me too, but I was 18 and didn't know it.

Mom would say how she couldn't tell a joke. And she couldn't.

"What'd the guy say to his mother?"

"Wife. What'd the guy say to his wife, Mon," someone would correct her.

But Mom could tell a story. And she could live one too. After her and Dad's divorce, she took me and my sister and we moved into Nana and Grandpa's second story flat on 18th and Church. My older cousin Nancy escorted us on a few field trips to Eureka Valley branch of the San Francisco Public Library. We got library cards, and I checked out *Green Eggs and Ham* and *Pierre*.

It was my sister who introduced me to the beauty and power of stories in books. I followed her into school by a year, and I wanted to be just like her. When we picked her up from kindergarten, she ran to Mom singing, *She'll be coming 'round the mountain when she comes* and I repeated *She'll pound the muffin when she runs*. Later, she retreated into the world of Harriet, her best friends Sport and Janie, and that notebook. I snuck a peek inside the book as soon as she set it down to wash dishes. When we were teenagers, she read then shared *Down These Mean Streets, Manchild in the Promised Land*, and other books that a neighbor not a librarian loaned her. I was blown away. Mom didn't seem to care what we read as long as we were reading.

One of my aunts was a reader. She had a new, fat, hard book every month. Mom didn't get books in the mail or check them out of the library. She bought magazines like *Jet* or *Newsweek* and read them in snatches of time between washing dinner dishes and getting ready for bed.

I remember looking from Nana and Grandpa's second story window and wanting to freeze the moment. Watching the shape-shifting clouds slowly form and reform, sometimes I wondered if it was really happening or a dream. I thought if I could capture it somehow, I would know. Whatever the feeling was, at the time I couldn't write much more than my name.

My first memory of writing—because I wanted to, because I thought I had a story to tell, and even to contribute to my relatives, and the family of books—I was around 9 years old sitting in our front bedroom facing Guerrero Street. We had all moved away from 18th and Church. Nana, Grandpa, and a couple of uncles lived next door—next door behind-the-wall not next door in the next building. An aunt and her family lived upstairs. I sat listening to four lanes of traffic speeding by. I got pen and paper thrilled to write my stories—playing at Mission Playground, walking to Sun Valley for a six pack of Pepsis, riding the school bus. I started to carve letters into paper then quickly stopped myself. I "remembered" that there were no books about brown girls who lived next to or downstairs from grandparents, aunts, uncles, and cousins on a busy street. I knew that people in books lived in houses. With a Mom and Dad. In a place that ended in -land. And they weren't girls or dark-skinned. They didn't have thick hair.

There was a boy...who lived in...England...no, Ireland I thought it sounded better...He lived with his mother and father...on a farm...They grew four-leaf clovers. I never finished the story.

I loved hearing stories as a child. Or overhearing them. I would stay sitting quietly in the corner or off to the side when the other kids ran out to play while the adults told each other stories about waiting at the bus stop, walking to work, sitting in a favorite bar, shopping on Mission Street.

After that first fiasco, I didn't try to write another story for a long time, but I did pick up a pencil again and kept a diary. Someone (Mom? a relative?) gave me a little green book with lined pages. The book locked. Of course, I lost the key. That stopped me for a while then I cut the binding and kept writing. I wrote in other notebooks off and on. I wanted to record, capture things. I didn't wonder if life was real or a dream as often.

Then as a junior at Mission High, Mr. Ruffner required daily journal entries in response to quotations such as "A journey of a thousand miles begins with a single step." I was in love with one of my best friends and needed to express it somewhere. I wrote cryptically about my love for Angel. I brought my journal home and warned my mother, "Don't read it."

"I don't want to read *that*," she replied so convincingly that it made me wish she did.

Then Mr. Ruffner invited a writer from California Poets in the Schools to lead us through poetry writing exercises. I wrote ambiguous poems and shared them with my friend I was in love with. She oohed and ahhhed. I wrote more. The writer typed up our poems and we became published poets. I was ready to write more, and I fantasized about publishing more. I didn't believe it would happen—just like my love for my friend—but I wanted it to.

It was around this time that I discovered the HQ section of the library, the section where the queer texts were shelved. For many years, I searched for a story similar to mine, a writer similar to me in those books, but I didn't find one.

I didn't know that there was a whole gay and lesbian world in the bars on 16th Street a few blocks away, Amelia's on Valencia. I was aware enough to know that the center of gay life moved from Polk to Castro Streets, but it was so male, so White. I wanted women like me.

My mother passed away after a sudden and quick illness during my first year of college and less than a year after our eviction from our Mission District flat. Hers followed two other relatives' recent deaths and a cousin close to my age died a few months after Mom. I didn't know what to do, so I went to live with my father and stepmother in the East Bay. I had previously spent plenty of weekends and a couple of summers with them, but I had always gone knowing I would return home to Mom. I bought a car and crossed the Bay Bridge to visit Mom at Holy Cross. Nana asked me to take her, but I never did. I selfishly went alone and talked and cried as I kneeled above her.

I dealt with the loss the same way I was dealing with my unrequited love. I wrote letters asking Mom why she left and to please come back. I wrote wondering about the eviction's role in her death, thinking it didn't play a role medically but knowing it did spiritually. I wrote down memories so I wouldn't forget anything about her. The wave of sadness enveloping my family jogged my memory of someone I had occasionally thought about over the years, my uncle who was killed when I was five years old.

After dropping out of SF State when Mom was first hospitalized, I signed up for classes at Chabot College. Eventually, I transferred to UC Berkeley. I double majored in English and History. Around this time, I found the essay "La Güera" by Cherríe Moraga. I read the author's bio and discovered she was teaching at Berkeley. I went to her office hours and in that first conversation I told her about my family, where I was from, that I wrote poetry. I'm sure I offered a disclaimer like I'm not a writer or the poems aren't any good, but she asked to see them anyway. I brought them to her and she returned them with comments. She named some of them what I had been too afraid to: lesbian. When I heard Sandra Cisneros was going to be a visiting faculty member, I signed up. I was very shy and unsure of myself, but I managed to write about Mom and home. Sandra and my classmates responded positively and encouraged me to keep writing.

Later when Cherríe facilitated a writing workshop off campus for lesbians of color, I joined. Then in 1992, she began a new workshop for Chicana, Latina, and Indigenous & Native women (Indígena as Scribe). Sessions were held in the Mission at Brava! for Women in the Arts' studio on the corner of 20th and Bryant Streets. My colleagues—women aged 20s to 60s, born within these borders and beyond, across the class and sexuality spectrums—reacted favorably to my poems and stories about my family and home.

I started meeting in informal writing groups with members from the workshop for women of color, Indígena, friends from Cal, and friends of friends. Sometimes we were all women, sometimes all queer, sometimes mixed. We took turns facilitating. We co-facilitated. We worked in different genres and even art forms. Some were filmmakers, painters, architects. But we all wanted to help each other fulfill our visions. And many of us were living, working, and performing in the Mission.

Then I decided to pursue an MFA in Creative Writing. I rounded up all the courage I had and applied to the college where I had started as a freshman before Mom got sick. I thought getting accepted would be coming full circle. State rejected me. I thought I had been a fool to dream. While working as an administrator for Brava, Joan Pinkvoss from Aunt Lute Feminist Press down the hall told me about a writing scholarship to the University of Iowa. Iowa's Writer's Workshop was then and is now considered one of this country's top writing programs. I knew that if State had rejected me, Iowa would too. Maybe the Workshop would've, but the scholarship was for the Nonfiction program. I applied and was accepted. Less than six months later, I was experiencing my first white winter.

In class after class, I read and heard many stories about White family life in suburbia. I was familiar with suburbia. It had been cultural shock to live there instead of just visit, but that's where Dad and my stepmother lived. When it was my turn to get workshopped (listen to our peers critique our work and critique isn't supposed to mean give negative feedback) for a story about my family, one of my peers commented that the narrator was trying to make the reader feel guilty. This was the same woman who wrote about a chandelier and piano in her livingroom as if it were common for everyone. I got tired of hearing how my people and land were "exotic." I considered leaving but decided I was getting that damn degree. I had the chance to stay for a PhD in English. I chose not to because I didn't want to study literature, I wanted to write it. Also, I feared it would kill my love for writing poems and stories. Even though some family members have asked me over the years about going back to school for a PhD, seeing how graduate school, especially doctorate programs, have affected friends, especially women of color, I have no regrets. And I'm so glad that I went to Iowa with some foundation built up in community-based groups and workshops.

I came home and started meeting in informal writing groups with friends again. They reminded me of my work's value and supported my development. But I went through long periods where I've not written, told myself I'm not a writer, I'm not going to write my stories, they don't matter. Let them go. Someone else will write them. Someone else should. Or they don't matter. I'd stop for a long time then get mad because I wasn't reading about my family, our streets. Even when I heard someone read about a Latino family in the Mission, I'd be frustrated because it wasn't *my* family.

A community resource that Ricardo Bracho and Jesse Johnson started, Proyecto ContraSIDA Por Vida based on 16th Street after a Dolores Street location, sparked a fire in many Queer Latinas/os and other People of Color throughout the Bay Area. And before PCPV there was CURAS Community in Response to AIDS SIDA with Diane Felix and other folks. Proyecto's primary objective was "to provide a safe space, programs and services that invigorate Latina/o bisexual, lesbian, transgender and gay gente in the San Francisco Bay Area with debate and desire, intellectual thought, erotic imagination and heartfelt passion." Many, many brilliant, talented, creative people gravitated to Proyecto. Professor Horacio Roque Ramírez, a gay Salvadoreño immigrant, wrote his dissertation on Queer Latino community in the Mission. He interviewed many people, including me. He knew about my writing and always encouraged me to write my stories, write my (this) book. Even when he was a stellar grad student and in-demand professor with an active social life, he remembered and encouraged me and my work.

I always felt my family and our community in general mattered. It bothered me that we were absent from history books or *The Chronicle* unless they were negative or inaccurate depictions. Or written by outsiders with a savior viewpoint. After too many years, here are some poems and stories based on my family's history in the Mission. I don't write to speak for anyone. I don't claim to have the truth or answers for anyone. Everyone has stories. They may choose to share them with only family or friends. Or not. But they have stories. These are my creative depictions, interpretations, presentations culled from my unreliable memory, old journals, and shared experiences. There was a graffiti artist who painted these ethereal horses and signed their name, Reminisce. There's some reminiscing going on in these pages, some nostalgia.

One thing I'm not nostalgic about is Mission Dolores. From the mission's website, "The Mission has been a steadfast witness to the span of San Francisco's history including the California Gold Rush... The Mission Cemetery is the final resting place of some 5,000 Ohlone, Miwok, and other First Californians who built Mission Dolores and were its earliest members and founders." Growing up, I heard 5,000 bodies were buried beneath Dolores Park. I didn't realize it was 5,000 *Native* bodies. The mission sits on such a small parcel of land those Native bodies must be under Mission Dolores, the basilica, Dolores Park, Mission High, and other areas.

When I write about my Mission, I'm talking about the people, the streets, the neighborhood. We didn't have much except each other and this place. Inside are some memories about them that have helped me arrive where I am today.

Cathy Arellano
Sacramento, California

Salvation
on Mission Street

"...I was writing my heart out. I was writing myself back in."

Lorna Dee Cervantes
"The Latin Girl Speaks of Rivers"
Sueño

Mission Walls

U.S. OUT OF EL SALVADOR
spray painted on Carl's Bakery

Estrella said,
"We had maids and a big house
before the Communists came"
She lived in the projects on Harrison
I didn't believe her
but I was still her friend

FMLN
on pillars of Everett Middle School

FSLN
on fence next to Bi-Rite

U.S. OUT OF NICARAGUA
on Anna's Danish Cookies' alleyside wall

when Uncle Auggie said
"I'm going to my meeting
with my Comité"
the rest of the adults in our house
who spoke Democrat
not Republican
not Sandinista
looked away

YANKEE GO HOME!
everywhere

I still wonder
if I'm Yankee
or Revolutionary

Free the Mission, Free Ramona

She opens the livingroom door. Her mother lays on the couch and watches Van Amburg and Jerry Jensen on the 11 o'clock news.

"I'm going, Ma."

Her mother nods as she pulls a Marlboro from the red box.

She searches for her girls in a pile on the carpet. They're tangled with their cousins. Her mother bathed and put all the girls to bed hours ago while she napped.

She steps quietly down the hall, down the stairs onto 18th Street. She looks for the 33. Cables are quiet.

She walks toward Mission Street on the high school side across from the park.

She crosses diagonally to the hippie restaurant on the corner. She notices the rainbow hovering over a forest mural on the Real Good Karma restaurant wall. She turns and scans the empty street for unwanted company. She passes tiny Oakwood alley then Bi-Rite where there's nothing right to buy there, but her family does everyday. She continues past Angie's Hair Salon.

Right before Carl's Bakery—

Police cruiser crashes over curb in front of her.
Fear ricochets through her body.
Cops jump out
"HALT
HANDS IN THE AIR
TOSS YOUR PURSE"

She wets herself
raises arms
tosses purse

One cop crouches behind cruiser's door with gun and headlights
pointed at her.

Officer near her dumps purse
out tumble couple dollar bills
random coins
wallet
expired bus transfers
large tortoise shell sunglasses
ball point pen
shaved eye pencil
compacts
comb
brush
lipsticks
lip brush
sticks of Double Mint
loose Kool Milds

He kicks contents until he sees her ID.

"Pick it up."

"What?"

"Pick up your damn card."

She does.

"Bring it to me."

She walks toward him. He stops her when she's arm's length's away.
He takes it from her hand.

"Stand where you were."

She backs up a few steps.

"Raymo-, Ruh-Ramona Are-ee-land-o. Did I say it right?"

She pauses then nods quickly. She sees her cigarettes strewn on the sidewalk, craves one.

"Ramona, where're you going this time of night?"

"Work."

"Work?"

Officer looks at his partner behind the car door. Second officer grins.

"Yes."

"And where do you work?" Second officer looks toward Mission Street. She can't see him. He smiles broadly.

"Post office. Rincon Annex."

"Where do you live?"

"Up 18th."

"Does your husband know you're out?"

"He knows I have to support our daughters," she answers without thinking.

"Does he know his wife's a smart ass?"

She doesn't say anything.

"So, you have children?"

"Yes."

"Where are they now?"

"My mother's."

Second officer turns his flashlight to the side of her face.
The glow of the red streetlight changes to green...yellow...red.
He moves the flashlight from her cheek
to her neck
over her breasts
down her thighs
on her groin.

Light clicks off.

"We apologize for any inconvenience," first officer states without
conviction.

He holds out her card. She hesitates then walks toward him. She
reaches for her ID.

"But you fit the description."

"I fit the what?"

"Have you heard about the fugitive Angela Davis?"

"No."

"You haven't heard of that—?!" second officer starts to ask.

"Paul!"

"I work and take care of my girls. I can't even remember the damn bus schedule."

"She's a member of the Black Panthers. She's responsible for the murder of officers of the law and an innocent civilian," first officer informs her.

He waits then asks, "Don't you have anything to say?"

"I didn't know."

"Well, we're onto her."

He pushes the card into her hand and walks back to the cruiser and climbs in the passenger side. His partner spits out the window and lurches back into the street.

She concentrates on slowing her breathing. She hunts for her purse then wallet and bends down when she sees them. She uses her purse like a dustpan to collect whatever belongings she can collect in one quick sweep. She straightens up then turns toward Mission Street.

She catches the 14 to the end of the line and walks into the Art Deco monstrosity. She shows her ID, punches in, and sits on a metal stool. For eight hours, she files envelopes according to zip code into library card catalogue-sized cubbies. She punches out and walks to the heavy door and pushes it open. The blast of sunlight shocks her back inside for a few seconds before she walks out. She catches the bus and retraces her steps from half a day and lifetime earlier. She lifts her head and sees in bold, block letters

FREE ANGELA
where once there was
FREE HUEY
FREE LOS SIETE

Over the years, when she sees
FREE INEZ
FREE DESSIE
FREE LEONARD
FREE NORMA JEAN

She prays for their release. Or escape.

Korean Vet Shot in Bar Argument

A veteran of Army service
        on Nana's mantel
        between the dipping bird
        and Auntie Ellie's graduation portrait
        above the oval mirror
        that eight-by-ten of him
        with sweet lashes
        dark honey skin
        inside beige uniform and cap
        bullet-black eyes and sure smile
        that don't reveal a single horror

in Korea
        a million miles away
        with thousands of other boys
        he survived the Cold War alone

was shot and killed
        husband
                of his third wife
        son
                who defended his mother
                from his father's blows
        father of three
                who cuddled his youngest daughter
                in burgundy quilt war souvenir
        brother
                who asked his four sisters
                after their break-ups
                if they were *sure*
                she didn't want him to *talk*
                to that asshole
        uncle
                who tickled nieces
                to steal back blanket

last night

        second night of new year
        second homicide of '71

in a Mission
District bar

        he grabbed kid brother
        home on leave
        pushed him down the stairs
        out of their parents' flat
        led him away from
        their mother's "Stop yelling, yous kids!"
        the kids' "She hit me!"
        their brothers' "Tackle!"
        for a game of pool
        coupla beers
        an hour of peace
        three blocks away

after an argument
over the war in Vietnam

        the war
        any war
        a bar stool
        song on the jukebox

Sonny Martinez,
28,

        twenty-fucken-eight

was pronounced dead

        no more smoking that smoke
        no more getting lost
        in Jimi's psychedelic riffs

at Mission Emergency Hospital
after the shooting
in the De Lux Bar
at 18th and Valencia Streets.

> Valencia to Guerrero
> Guerrero to Dolores
> Dolores to Church

Police Sgt. Ed Epsting said
witnesses reported
the argument but were
unclear which side Martinez had
taken in the dispute.

> this side, that side
> right side, wrong side

Martinez was shot in the chest
with a .32 caliber pistol.

> "Mama, Mama" as his head knocked
> on wooden bar before slipping
> between two stools
> "stay with me, man"
> brother cooed to brother

Epsting said a description
supplied by witnesses led to
J—— T——, who lived
nearby and was found in
another tavern
in the neighborhood.
T—— was booked on
suspicion of murder charges.

the blood that splashed into floorboards
soaked through earth
dripped into Our Lady of Sorrows waters
joined five hundred years
of blood flowing beneath Mission Dolores

we have been attacked
in body and soul
we have been denied justice
and pushed out
but we will always
be connected
to this land
these waters

We Say Happy New Year's Instead of Feliz Navidad

Growing up, New Year's was my family's biggest holiday. Not enough of us went to church for Easter and Christmas could become too expensive trying to shop for everyone. The adults seemed to have an agreement that they were excused from buying presents for everyone else's kids. They had grown up receiving an orange or apple on Christmas so there was little tradition to break once nieces and nephews arrived.

But New Year's was a time to celebrate. All we needed was each other, food, drinks, and music. The first ingredient was always available and we just increased the other three.

Nana was the lone cook every night of the year and was very content to be the only one chopping or stirring, but on New Year's Eve she drafted her four daughters to help her. Cooking on New Years was so special that only the big girls Nancy and Lola—dish washers, not dish dryers—could help.

One time, me, Dede, Marlene, and Denise took turns passing by the table spread with ojas and pots and pans and spoons and pinched off small balls of masa. We carried them outside and pretended to make our own tamales and have our own party. Then Dede got the idea to play Masa Dodge Ball. Uncle Sammy was going to the store to buy more beer and saw us. When he got back, he said we had to go and stay inside the livingroom. We went in but we still had some masa. Dede had another idea. She threw her masa up at the ceiling. We saw her masa stick then we all threw our leftover masa until one corner of the livingroom ceiling resembled the top of a cave. That was so fun until Uncle Sonny banged open the door.

"What the hell's going on in here?"

"She made me," Denise said.

"Made you what?" he asked as he scanned the room.

We nervously stayed quiet.

"I'm going to kick your asses if you mess with her shit. You little shits."

Then we had to play hand games super quietly so he wouldn't knock on our heads.

Later, Uncle Auggie came in and played his Catch game with us. He pulled out a huge, empty mayonnaise jar filled with change. He held it high and opened the lid. After he turned the jar over, we scrambled, scraped, and clawed until each of us had our own mound of quarters, nickels, dimes, and pennies in front of us.

"I'm rich! I'm rich!" we yelled swirling our hands through our coins and grabbing handfuls then letting them rain down.

Then Nana came in and told us to go back outside until she called us.

Nana divided the chores amongst her daughters. Auntie Maggie was in charge of making sure there were plenty of nicely soaked ojas. She had to make sure there wasn't any corn silk hiding between the leaves before putting them in tubfuls of warm water. If that happened, then it would take a long time to pluck the wet and sticky "hairs."

Auntie Daisy had the job of spreading the masa on the hojas. She had to be careful to spread it thick enough to hold the meat sauce but not too thick so our tongues caught in a gooey masa mess. Nana wanted her tamales large, meaty, *and* juicy.

Mom often made plans to visit a nightclub or two during the evening, though always promising to return by the midnight countdown. Before she could leave for a club or even dance in the livingroom, she had to fulfill her responsibility to Nana. Mom was in charge of spooning the mole into the masa-covered hojas. She had to make sure there was a proportionate amount of meat to olives to sauce. No one likes dry or oliveless tamales. The hardest part was folding the hojas without spilling the mole, but Mom was a pretty good tamal folder. She was the second oldest and stepped in to assist Auntie Ellie who was Nana's number one assistant.

Auntie Ellie drove in from Pacifica for the day. Her job was to follow Nana around the kitchen and obey her orders as soon as she issued them. Auntie Ellie spent the whole time saying, "Mande, Ma. Mande." Nana followed no written recipe. It was "Put another spoonful of manteca into the masa" here or "Don't over fry the chicharrones" there. The chicharrones were our hors d'oeuvres until the main course was done steaming.

Nana's job was the hardest, of course. She oversaw her daughters, the food on the stove, and the rest of the house. Nana shopped, diced, poured, mixed, and cooked 100 pounds of masa from Mi Rancho and 100 pounds of meat from Lucky Pork for almost 24 hours making hundreds of tamales for the new year. She timed it just right so that the first batch would finish between 11:30 p.m. and midnight.

After the tamales, the best part of New Year's was the countdown. Then, someone turned off Nana's stereo that was encased in a large, wooden box and switched the TV onto "Dick Clark's Rockin' Eve." It was around this time that Auntie Maggie's kitchen duties were finished and she brought out bags of what she had hidden all night.

"Here, here, here," Auntie Maggie said as she pressed confetti, streamers, and noisemakers into each pair of cupped hands.

"Hey, I need a hat!"

"Barrel, pass that to Uncle Sammy!"

"Auntie Maggie, Auntie Maggie, can I have some more of the little paper?"

"What little paper?"

"Confetti, Mag, confetti!"

"Somebody turn the TV louder!"

With everybody standing, we shouted in unison, "10!"

"Where's your Nana?"

"9!"

"Nana!"

"I meant go get her! Ma!"

"8!"

"7!" Everybody would have their fists raised ready to scatter the colorful paper.

"6!" Nana would come hurrying from the kitchen.

"5!"

"4!"

"3!" I made sure that I was next to Mom.

"2!"

"1!"

"*HAP-PY* New Year's!" We'd throw our confetti in the air then us kids swept the carpet with our hands and piled it up and threw it at each other all over again. Then it was time to do what we rarely ever did: hug and kiss. And the adults did what I only saw Mom do very late some nights, cry.

While us kids were playing, Nana and Mom and the aunties pulled the steaming tamales from the huge pots and served everyone before they finally sat, ate their tamales, and drank cold Pepsis. After the confetti and tamales, Mom was the first to snap off the TV and blast the stereo. New Year's wasn't the time for her slow heartbreaking R&B songs she listened to after shouting on the phone to her boyfriend and it wasn't the time for the uncles'

> *All by myself*
> *I don't wanna be*
> *Alllll byyyyy myyyyy-sellllf*

Or

> *Louie Louie Louie Louie*
> *Louie Louie Lou-I*
> *Louie Louie Louie*
> *Louie Louie, you're gonna cry*

And not even

> *I'm not in love*
> *Requesting silence*

She didn't let the uncles play their super-long Santana solo songs either.

This was time for her Saturday morning throw-open-the-windows-and-greet-the-world music. Mom attached plastic, three-armed yellow discs to the small records, removed them off for the big ones. She didn't play any song more than once. People didn't seem to care what came from the speakers or how loud. Folks heard Stevie Wonder's "Awwwwww, if you really loved me" and Mom had her own "Soul Train."

Mom viewed everyone as potential dance partners and she had plenty to choose from. She loved to dance and she was "on the floor" almost every song.

After dancing up a storm, Mom would put on some music for Nana--Javier Solis, Antonio Aguilar, Flor Silvestre, Amalia Mendoza, José Alfredo Jiménez, and even Nat King Cole singing in Spanish. Hardly anyone danced to these but they raised their drinks to them.

"Come on, mija, dance with me," Mom often pleaded with Marlene or me.

I knew that after midnight with so many other people around, Mom couldn't make me dance with her.

"Oh, come on," she'd say with a big goofy grin showing the slight gap between her front teeth. But her feet moved too fast for me to follow and it wasn't just her feet. Her shoulders, hands, and hips all moved at the same time. They moved so well together that it seemed like the music followed her instead of her following the music.

I didn't like dancing with Mom. She wasn't Mom when she danced. She was a fancy lady with her hair and make-up done just right, wearing her hot pink silk blouse and cream-colored polyester slacks. I felt like Diana Ross was pulling me onstage. Sometimes, friends of the uncles seemed to think Mom was Diana Ross too and they tried to cut in if she was dancing with Dinky, Harpo, Cheeks, or one of the other little kids. Mom would just pick up the kid and walk away saying, "Some people just want to dance when they dance."

"To the left and back, to the right and back, mija," she tried to convince me, making her dancing sound as easy as the Hokey Pokey. "No, Mom," I'd tell her.

"Cómo friegas, muchacha," she'd say. If she was friega-ing me then I knew she wouldn't ask me too much longer.

Uncle Manny or Uncle Auggie were her best chances for dancing. They might resist for a little while, but eventually they'd say, "Aw, what the hell!" and join her on the dance floor.

New Year's was when we played and ran around and the adults didn't say No. The bold ones of us snuck sips of forgotten drinks. Sometimes after emptying a Pepsi bottle with a few sips of caramel syrup leftover, we gagged on ashes. When we got tired of scooping up used confetti or seeking clean Pepsis, us girls fell asleep wherever someone wouldn't step on us.

Burra Takes A Bath

When Nana bathed us kids, it felt like we were a bunch of beans. She'd yank one of us into the tub while there was water streaming from the spout before she plugged the drain. *If* she plugged the drain. Then she hunted our bodies for filth as diligently as she inspected her beans for rocks. She scoured our young feet, legs, bellies, arms, necks, and ears as if she were scrubbing excess dirt from her beans. She wasted no time as she rinsed off soap and shampoo. Nana could pull one child from the tub with her left hand and pull another in using her right. Our tears didn't slow her down one second. After the bath, it wasn't any easier.

"Burra, what have I told you about this mop?" She'd hiss, clutching a handful of our long hair.

"I'm not a donkey," we'd mutter. "Ow!"

"Stop moving, tonta" she'd demand with a rap on the head from the hard, pink, plastic Avon brush.

Sometimes it wasn't the combing or prickling but Nana knocking her knuckles on our head that made us stand still. Mom and the aunties and uncles said we had it easy.

"Nana used to throw or hit us with a shoe or hanger."

"A shoe, Mom?" I asked.

"There were nine of us. She didn't fool around."

Spanish Eyes

Bluuuuuue
Spanish eyes
Prettiest eyes in all of Mexico-o-o-o-o-o
Truuue Spanish eyes...

"Sing it, Engelbert!"

Please smile for me
Once more before I
Go-o-o-o!

Mama joined the man's voice playing on the stereo while she pulled
half a head of lettuce with brown edges from the fridge.

A plastic arm with a tiny spear slid to the center of the forty-five
then retreated. Another black disc clicked down the short silver
stick. The plastic arm returned and crackled at the smooth edge.

A violin stuttered. Mama set the mop against the wall
stretched her right arm while sawing it with her left hand.

I put down my teddy bear and copied her. She nodded to me.

"Sí, mija."

Someday!
We'll be together
Ah, say it say it say it say it again!

Diana and her Supremes hummed. Mama pressed her lips tight and
hummed.

You're far away from me, my love

Mama closed her eyes.

Arellano

"Mama, why you close your eyes?"

"I can hear the song better with my eyes shut. I'll be right back."

She plucked a tissue on her way out of the room and came back with a basket of clean laundry. She folded my big brothers' chonis and matched my big sister's socks. She tossed the last one without a partner at me.

"Mija, I need to rest. Go get a toy, a quiet one, and lay down with me."

She laid down on her big bed. She patted the space next to her. I laid down. She turned the radio dial to KDIA Lucky 13.

I clicked my Viewfinder over and over. Rudolph's tears hung frozen in the air. He leaped in slow motion to the front of Santa's sleigh. Lions, tigers, and elephants silently stalked each other on another disc.

Each day through my window
I watch her as she passes by

turned into

...showers...high of...
...crash on...exit closed until...
...hijackers...airplane...
...Zodiac...wanted...
...draft...boys...

Mama woke up and turned off the radio.

"I have to mail a bill. Put on your shoes and socks."

"Which sock goes on which foot?"

"Ay!"

At 17th and Mission, I spun around the pole beneath the 4 Wheel Tire sign. The 4 Wheel Tire sign spun above me.

"4 like me, like me! 4, 4, 4!"

We walked to the post office in the back of Bell Bazaar then back up Mission. At the uniform shop, we turned up 19th and walked past Jim's store to Judy's and Roy's. I wiggled free from Mama's grip, hopscotched over red sparkly sidewalk lines, unclicked my barrette and dropped it to mark my place.

"Mama, when's the boys' turn?"

"Turn for what?"

"The draft."

"What?"

"The radio said. The radio said all boys have to-"

"They're boys! They're *just* boys!"

She crossed her eyebrows at me and came closer. I jumped back from her twisted mouth. She grabbed my wrist. My free hand pointed to the sidewalk.

"My barrette, Mama! My barrette!"

She lifted my arm until I was hopping like a clumsy kangaroo.

"Ow, Mama, my arm!" I said pushing away from her.

"Godddd bless America!" she hissed.

She let my arm go, plucked a tissue from her coat pocket, and held her nose.

She peered over my head, up 19th Street toward Dolores Park. Past the bell, past the Father Hidalgo statue.

"I want Daddy."

"Daddy's at work," she said before bending her head lower. "Come here."

I didn't move. She picked up my barrette and held her hand open. She wiped her nose, squinted down at me and wiggled her fingers to call mine. She kneeled to my level.

"They're just boys. And you're just a little girl. Now, give me your hand. We're going home."

Don't Forget

After the big kids came home from school
after Nana rolled a pile of tortillas
to eat with her beans and rice
after we washed dried and put away dinner dishes,
he donned his brim, settled his weight on his good leg,
held his bum arm against his belly and said, "Let's go, mijas."

Five little girls hooted and hollered
danced and hopped
"Poppp!" an uncle whined.
"Mijas! Get your sweaters and meet me downstairs."

We ran to the hall closet, grabbed any sweater
and flew down like little drunk vultures.

"Hold hands."
Me, my sister, and sistercousins
laced fingers and raced up 18th Street to Joe's.

First one there twisted silver knobs,
lifted flaps, dipped fingers for free surprises
before horde pushed her away
then we all ran inside
almost knocking down Grandpa at the counter
in front of the ice creams.

"Line up over there."
Our hive buzzed over to soft wooden floor
nailed down before the quake.
We panted in front of the magic machine.

"Tell Joe what you want...Youngest first."
Joe pulled a green and snow-white
penguin paper cup.

"Grape!" "Cherry!" "Cherry!"
The choir rumbled.

"Mixed"
Dede ordered, silencing us with her boldness.

George pushed buttons
on a huge, noisy box
black numbers on white cards popped up
in a window at the top
a drawer popped out at the bottom
then he tapped the last numbers
into a small, quiet machine
that spit out two papers.

He handed both to Grandpa
Who kept one, signed the other
then returned it to George
who taped it on the back wall
with the rest.

We slurped down 18th Street
skipping then racing
happy for shots of sugar anything
thrilled not to share something.

Grandpa shouted into the wind
at our backs, "Don't forget!
You're Yaqui!"

New Year's 1983

"Dance with me, mija," Mom gently commanded, as Eydie Gorme sang "Luna Lunera."

I didn't resist. She pulled my limp arm up from the couch, raised my hands in hers, stepped toward me then back and repeated.

"Now you with me," she guided. I watched her feet leading me around Nana's livingroom.

"Look up, Catherine. Don't watch my feet," Mom said as she gently lifted my chin and we skirted aunts, uncles, and cousins sitting on sofa, loveseat or just standing around.

I awkwardly searched for her rhythm.

"Mom, see? I can't."

"Shhh shhh," she said smiling into my eyes and calming me down.

I wished I could dance to her beat though as much as I was stumbling, it felt good to dance with Mom. I never could match her rhythm. It didn't matter. She was glad I tried and I was glad to have her all to myself. There was a bunch of family around—not as many as usual—but none of my siblings that night. And not her boyfriend and not the girl I was in love with.

It felt like the war between us had come to an end. I had been an obedient Mama's girl for most of my 18 years. Sure, I had gotten high, had a few drinks, cut a few classes, fooled around with a couple of boys. And fallen head over heels in love with a girl. But I had graduated from high school and was in college.

It was a strange and hard time. Even though it had been a few years since Grandpa had been admitted to Laguna Honda and Uncle Paul and Auntie Maggie had divorced, I knew they were around. Then Uncle Paul died and soon after Grandpa too. There hadn't been a death in the family since Uncle Sonny a little more than ten years earlier.

Mom had been sick off and on for weeks. Her being sick and not going out dancing like she usually did on New Year's was strange. So was celebrating our first New Year's in a distant, foggy corner of the Mission.

Dolores Park, Our Backyard

"Go play at the park, yous kids.
Where I can see yous,"
Nana ordered.

"WHERE SHE CAN SEE YOU!"
Uncle Davy barked.

"Yeah, OK."

"WHAT?"

"Yes."

"And empty your shoes before
yous come back.
I don't want any sand on my floors."

"YOU HEAR HER?
NO SAND."

"Yes, Nana.
Yes, Uncle."

We grabbed sweaters.
We ran downstairs.

"DON'T RUN."

We stopped running.
We crashed into each other.

"Hold hands when you cross the street."

"HOLD HANDS."

"Hey, don't step on my foot.
I didn't mean to.
Don't push me."

"NO FIGHTING."

We froze.
Nancy opened the wood-frame glass door.
She pulled us out
by hand, arm, shoulder, collar.

Denise and me held the swirling black wrought iron rail,
all the way down.
Dede and Marlene pushed off the rail and
flew down the speckled stairs.
Our mob of little girls floated to the corner
a few feet away.
Fingers twined, palms clasped.

"I don't want you."
Palms pushed away.
"Who said I wanted you?"
until sisters cupped cousins' palms.

Nancy watched light
stepped off curb
looked left
right
left
waved us forward.

When we crossed 18th street
our eyes followed
the aroma of sizzling grease
to Dyn-A-Mite.

We felt our empty pockets
turned away.

We waited for the light
waited for Nancy
she repeated her duty.
We crossed Church Street
and tightroped the concrete island.
We finished the obstacle course
by crossing the streetcar tracks.

I ran to the empty waiting room
of the white bungalow.

"My fort," I claimed.

"My dream house," Denise declared.
"No, mine."
"Mine."

"Get over here!"
Nancy grabbed Denise's arm.
I followed.

We picked miniature red apples from bushes,
smashed them using mangled gate lock handle.
We dipped invisible spoons into bowled hands,
feasted on mush.

Index fingers and thumbs gripped
delicate teacup handles.
Pinkies pointed up
just like on the cartoons.

I wandered away
sat on the grass.

"Sit right," Dede said.
"I am."
"Your legs are open."
"What?"

"Girls should sit like this"
(her index and middle finger together)

"Or like this"
(her middle finger over index)

"Girls who sit like this"
(her index and middle spread wide)

"Get this"
(her thumb between index and middle finger)

"Like this!"
(her thumb and middle finger snap!)

"What's that?"

"If you don't know,
I can't tell you"
then she ran away.

I found Nancy
picked daisies with her.
She showed me how to split stems
thread one into the other.
We slipped on our bracelets.
She held a necklace above me

then a whee-o-wheeeet whistle blew!!!

All five of our heads snapped
to Nana's second story window.
We saw a white t-shirt
sitting at the large, wood frame.

We dropped jewelry
            teacups
                    saucers
                            bowls.

We walked to the corner
                held hands
                        crossed street
                                climbed stairs.

Nancy opened the door.

"Dinner's ready!
Wash your hands!"

"USE SOAP"

We raced up the inside stairs.

"DON'T RUN
How many times do I have to-?!"

We stopped.
Slowly quietly
we lifted one leg
then the other.

"Yous better not have brought that park
into my house!"

We stopped
checked the bottoms of our shoes.

"Come and eat, you fuchi girls."

BRT: Beans, Rice, Tortillas

Stinkie, Bones, Melón, and Barril! These were some of Grandpa's nicknames for his granddaughters. Sometimes when I entered a room that he was already in, he sang, "Roll out the barrel/ We'll have a barrel of fun" and kept time by patting his leg or conducting an orchestra with his invisible baton in the air. Once when us kids were sitting on the floor watching his favorite Saturday evening TV program, "The Lawrence Welk Show," Cindy and Bobby, two of the show's regular dancers, glided around the stage while a famous person sang my song. Oom-pa-pa!

No one else had their own song, but almost everyone had a nickname. Her real name was Frances, but Grandpa called Nana, Franky. His five sons grew up answering to Chippy and Chepo. Nana's sister, Auntie Donna, couldn't remember all of Nana's 20-plus grandkids' names and called us all Sam. Our five uncles called us whatever they felt like. We ranged in age from Nancy's ten down to mine and Denise's five to Dinky, Markie, and Stephie's one or two years old.

When one of the adults called us, we answered: "What?"

They'd say: "'What?'! Don't tell me 'What?' Say 'Mande.'"

Grandpa, Nana, Mom, the aunties, and uncles tried to teach us to say "Mande" but it was hard. They never commanded us to command them.

At the end of 1970, five of Nana and Grandpa's nine children had married, had their own kids, divorced, and returned to their parents' home, a rented flat across from Mission High. Kitty corner to Dolores Park. Almost every night their other children who didn't live in the flat came over for dinner. Auntie Ellie and Uncle Sal drove in on the weekends with Lola, Freddy, and JJ. From the big window in the diningroom, we could see Auntie Maggie or Uncle Paul pushing Stephanie in her stroller when they walked over from a few blocks away.

Nana made sure that whoever was sitting down in the diningroom, livingroom, on the floor, or standing up at 5 o'clock ate a good meal and that meant eating some of her beans. Dinner was Nana's beans, Spanish rice, tortillas, and something else. The something else was usually cuts of meat that if laid next to each other added up to whole pieces sold by Lou the Butcher at Busy Bee. There were enough nights when there was no something else.

I don't know what made white rice with tomato sauce "Spanish," but that's what Nana called it so that's what we called it. First, Nana poured oil in one of her cast iron pots. Once it was hot, she poured from the Mahatma bag. Soon after, there was that toasted rice smell. She'd have taken a break from pushing the rice around with one of her tall, blue, speckled spoons to open a small can of Del Monte tomato sauce. She'd pour a can then fill it with water from the faucet a few times. Then she'd sprinkle some salt and pepper and leave it alone until her tortillas were ready.

Nana's tortillas were flour, never corn. And they weren't just homemade but handmade. There was no wooden press in Nana's kitchen. She mixed flour and manteca in the huge, low and wide, green Tupperware bowl. It transformed from sticky blob to integrated mass. She'd pinch a small handful and roll it with a dash of flour in her hands. Magically within seconds, lightly dusted ping pong ball-sized spheres appeared. She set these orbs to the side in a simple line then rows of even number to wait their turn for the comal. She lifted an orb and rolled north then south, turned the world east, rolled new section north and south. She repeated until enough rotations had transformed dough as close to tortilla as possible without heat. By this time, she had already turned on the flame beneath her trusted flat, circle of iron. When it was ready, she laid the raw dough upon her comal more gently than she ever tucked any of us kids into bed. She used a folded dish towel to subdue the rising dough. Then she lifted and flipped over. She pressed and turned a few times then lifted and piled the tortilla in another dish towel. As the tortillas cooked, the stack opened and closed to receive the new additions. Nana didn't ever seem to make enough. Truth is, there was no way she could ever make enough. There were too many of us and they were too delicious.

There were always plenty of beans though. String beans, lima beans, French cut beans—those were beans, but they weren't *beans*. Pinto beans—boiled or refried with bacon drippings, topped with Monterey Jack cheese when we had it—were for breakfast, lunch, and dinner. Nana called them frijoles, but we knew she meant beans. As the years passed and we kept calling them beans and not frijoles, so did she. Nana eventually gave up telling us her other words, including leche, agua, cilantro, pan, and trapo.

We heard the Brady kids ask their mother Carol or Alice the maid "What's for dinner?" but when we asked Nana she said, "Caca! And you're going to eat it!"

Mornings started with beans tumbling onto Nana's kitchen table. Then there was the slide and swish as she swirled them closer to her to inspect for rocks. Then it was the rat-a-tat-tat'ing rainfall of beans hitting the bottom of her stainless steel bean pot that was resting in her lap. She added water from the faucet at the beginning, but from then on she used the water from a tea kettle that she kept on a low simmer and refilled throughout the process.

"Why you use water from the stove not the faucet?" I asked her once.

"So they don't turn dark," she answered.

Years later, when her daughters rented their own homes and cooked their own meals, us kids made sure our mothers followed Nana's steps. It didn't matter because their beans didn't taste like Nana's beans.

Arellano

"Your beans aren't as good as Nana's," me or Marlene told Mom just like Nancy, Dede, and Denise told Auntie Daisy.

"I know, I know, but you still have to eat them," they replied never disagreeing.

Their beans weren't awful. They just weren't Nana's. They could fry up some bacon and throw in some Monterey Jack cheese for passable refried beans. But when it came to fresh beans out of the pot, there was no contest. We wanted Nana's beans. Somebody might get the last bowlful, probably Uncle Sammy, but she would already have a new pot simmering on the stove.

Dolores Park Horses

Peeking out Nana's second story window
we saw two policemen on horses
at the 33 Ashbury stop
waiting like they were going to clop aboard
when the bus sailed down from the Castro
on thick MUNI wires.
Horse and riders bobbed into the park,
maintaining a beat slower
than the conga rhythm
coming from the other side.
When the horses disappeared,
the music stopped.

The uncles took turns
sitting behind heavy binoculars
with *The Chronicle* in their laps.
"We found your horse, Ma. Ha, ha."
The uncles blew whit-whee-o whistles
across Church Street tracks
to Mission co-eds.
Necks to thighs
filled the double glass view.
Some of the girls glanced up,
didn't turn away.

Ten-year old Janet
who lived around the corner
and ran faster than any kid
forgot her shoes at the park.
She ran back quicker than she could sing
My mother, your mother
lived across the Bay
but not swifter than monster arms
could reach from bushes.

Arellano

After that, Janet leaned on her mama
while she walked bowlegged
to the store and back
before they galloped away
in their U-Haul.

Casanova

"Just a few," we said when we entered hours ago. That night it was just us—me, my girlfriend Sonia, and Uncle Manny.

We were just "having a few" and "shooting the shit," as Uncle liked to say. We played pool and I tried to make the games interesting, but it made me remember why I didn't ever sign my name up on the chalkboards to play in the dyke bars.

"Monica! You're beautiful," Uncle Manny told the bartender behind the counter.

He was handsome in his plain white t-shirt and grey slacks with his neatly trimmed mustache. I knew there was Tres Flores from its stout, flowery bottle in his hair and Old Spice from a tall ship on a cream-colored bottle on his cheeks. I'm sure if I asked, I'd find out that he sprayed his pits with a tan can of Right Guard. Uncle kept it simple whether sitting on a barstool, going to work at Hostess Bakery on Bryant, or watching the Giants or 49ers at home.

"Have I introduced you to the...the...this...bar...bartender?" Uncle Manny asked with a tilt to his head as he pointed the cue stick at Monica.

Before I could answer, he added, "Monica, this is my niece Barr" then his lips struggled to pronounce, "Ca-...What's your name? Cath-ee-rin?"

I'd never heard Uncle say my birth certificate name, my bill collector name. The one Dad uses and Mom used rarely.

"Martinez, you don't even know your own niece's name? Is she your niece?"

"I'm his niece. You can call me Cathy," then I pushed the cue stick through my left fingers resting on the green felt.

"Monica's the prettiest, baddest-assed bartender in the Mission," he told me for the tenth time. "She won't marry me. Did I tell you that?"

Sonia happened to be standing near the corner pocket where he was aiming. Right before Uncle Manny released his cue stick, she wiggled her ass.

He finally made a mistake and knocked in one of my balls.

"Barrel! Sonia used her secret weapon!"

"Damn you, Sonia," Uncle Manny said happily surprised with Sonia's strategy.

"Don't blame her for your shitty shots, Martinez," Monica said having missed the wiggle.

"Shitty shots?! Damn you too, Monica! Get me a shitty shot! One for each of us!" he twirled his finger in the air.

"Be nice, Martinez," Monica told him and added, "He's usually such a gentleman."

"Aw, go to hell," Uncle said flipping her off and turning away.

"Geez, Uncle," I said and grimaced at Sonia, remembering that I met her in a Women's Studies class.

"Wait until you meet the men in my family," Sonia whispered to me as she passed on her way to the jukebox.

"Don't be an asshole in front of your niece, Manny," Monica said in a serious tone that didn't match her smiling face.

"I love you, Monica. Marry me tonight," he pleaded.

"I swear this guy..." shaking her head and laughing.

"Go to hell then!"

"Kiss my ass!" she responded and strolled down to get our shots at the other end of the bar.

"Come back here and I will!...Agh, pour yourself one too. On me. I mean I'll pay, but if you want to pour—!"

"Uncle!"

Monica mouthed "Dream on" to Uncle then turned her back to him.

"I'll be in my office," Uncle Manny said as he turned toward the men's room.

I joined Sonia at the jukebox and punched in some Al Green, Aretha Franklin, Marvin Gaye, and a few others. Mom always had the livingroom cabinet shelves filled with stacks of LPs and 45s. There were always so many records around that my sister and I learned to see a flash of color and know the record company. Blue with a road map on top was Motown, yellow with brown on top was TAMLA, red with black writing was usually Atlantic, but sometimes they used yellow. Then we learned the songs on each label and we'd play "Name That Tune" with our cousins. We beat them every time, always guessing the song in less than three notes, sometimes just one: "Dis..." "Distant Lover Marvin Gaye!" we'd shout.

After Sonia loaded up the jukebox with her favorites, I chose a few songs I remembered Uncle Manny playing on repeat when he lived with us, Santana's "One Chain," Gloria Gaynor's "I Will Survive," and Prince's "Purple Rain." Then I added Aerosmith's "Dream On" for fun. Sonia and I started walking to the pool table, then turned when we saw him sitting at one of the bar's small tables. There were three empty shot glasses on the table.

He seemed to be talking to himself. We sat down.

"Your mother. Very good woman," he said sighing, facing me with his eyes closed.

Without thinking about it, I let out a big sigh. Then my eyes started to water. It had been almost fifteen years and that quick I was in pain again.

"Yeah, Uncle, she was," I could feel Sonia's eyes on me and turned away.

Sonia reached for my hand. I stroked her palm with my thumb.

"Is good woman. Not was," he said looking right at me.

"Yes, Uncle. Is. She is. It's just—"

"Beut-fool person," he added. He turned his head to the side and closed his eyes.

He missed her. I missed her. Sometimes it was just worse than others for us. The doctors never could tell us exactly why. They just knew what: her liver and kidneys stopped working. Forty-five and she was in and out of the hospital in a month.

"Yeah, pretty lady," I said as I nodded my head.

"I goddamn love that woman," Uncle Manny mumbled then turned to Sonia. "My sister...helluva woman," he said as he pulled his left brown man hand up to his squinting eyes.

"Good times. Your Momnme."

He flexed his right arm, pointed from his chest to the space just to the right of him, in and out, in and out. I could almost see her there. I squeezed Sonia's hand.

"'Hey, Manny the Man,' she'd say," he remembered. "Or just 'Man.' She called me Man," he giggled.

His giggles fizzled to mumbles.

"Aw, shit," his hand fell to his side.

Monica cocked her head to the side and raised her eyebrows. I waved that he was okay.   I remembered his "Man's." I remembered my "Mija's."

Mission Be Safe

"Hurry up!" Nancy told us near the bungalow as we left the park.
"That man behind us is IT and if he tags you you're gonna be IT."

We held hands crossing the street not caring if we were holding our
sister's hand.

Nancy pushed our backs
to hurry us up the curb.
We grabbed the streetlight pole,
our base when we played tag.

The man followed.

Nancy swatted us along 18th
and up the stone steps.
Dede flung open the front door
and we flopped in.
We scrambled over each other
up the inside stairs
like baby rats hunting for mama's milk.

Nancy slammed the front door.

"WHAT THE HELL ARE YOU KIDS—?"

We heard Uncle Davy march
from the kitchen to the stairs.
He leaned over the banister.

"He's IT!
The man's IT!"
we yelled climbing the stairs
and ducking Uncle's knuckles
swinging to knock on our heads.

Up to the landing
then left to the kitchen
to Nana.

"There's a man chasing us,"
Nancy said pointing down the stairs.

We heard the door open
footsteps coming up the stairs.

"Goddamnmotherfucker!"
Uncle Davy leaped down.

The door opened and slammed.
Uncle Davy followed.
He returned twisting his ring
with magenta stone in flat side.

"Get over here, you girls!"

We lined up.

Uncle Davy jabbed
in front of our five noses
with his index finger and pinky
"That's why we tell you
play where we can see you
come when we call you
don't talk to strangers."

"We didn't ta—"

"Hey!"

The next day they grabbed two of us.
Sent us to the store for Italian salami,

Arellano

French's mustard, a loaf of Kilpatrick's,
and a bag of plain Laura Scudder's.
Told us
"Be careful.
Hold hands."

When we got to the bottom of the stairs,
one of them hollered
"Come back!"

We ran back up.

"Get a six pack of Pepsis too.
Don't forget to take back the empties.
And make sure the door is unlocked."

Queen Nancy

Grandpa and Nana's flat on 18th Street had two bedrooms. I have no idea where Mom and Auntie Daisy slept. I guess it helped that Mom was working the night shift at the post office and slept during the day. Grandpa slept in his own room on a four poster bed, framed by four wood-carved bulging domes, that sat solidly in the center. There was a tall, five-drawer bureau set along one wall.

Behind the livingroom double doors, the uncles' room was painted with posters. There was one of two guys with thick wavy hair, like Uncles Sonny and Sammy, riding motorcycles. A couple of Bruce Lees. He wore a claw scratch on his stomach in one, sunglasses and a lace-up shirt in another. Pages torn from the *Playboy* magazines stuffed under the bathtub were taped on their headboards. And there was one poster of a man playing a guitar who resembled one of the guys who played music every day in the park. My uncles shared twins and a rollaway that was unfolded only at night. Uncle Sonny and his two-year old Dinky, covered themselves with Nana's burgundy quilt. Nana claimed the livingroom couch for herself and Markie.

Me, Nancy, Dede, Denise, and Marlene made our bed on the livingroom floor. Every night, we pulled the sheets, Army blankets, and Nana's colorful crocheted blankets from the chest in the hall closet. We girls worked together in two assembly lines on either side of our square of space holding our covers by the corners, throwing them into the air, then letting them fall like parachutes across the carpeted floor. Every night, one of us couldn't forget the shiny burgundy quilt still in the closet.

"Nana, can we use—" one of us would start to ask.

And every night she told us, "Put that down! Yous girls know better. It's for your Uncle Sonny and Dinky. He's watching his TV program. Now yous go to bed."

We knew better, but we tried to fool her: a woman who survived Grandpa's violent years, raised nine of her own children, and was helping to raise half her grandchildren. We never slept with the silky cover. After failing to get the burgundy quilt, we would move onto our nightly fight: Which three of us five would sleep in the sacred middle and be warm all night?

"I'm the oldest," Nancy said well aware of the role age played in our family's hierarchy of power.

"I'm the youngest," Denise piped up.

I knew that Denise and I were born in the same year. "I'm the youngest too." If she could claim youngest, why not me?

"You're the chubbiest," my sister Marlene liked to remind me as if I didn't know why Grandpa had nicknamed me Barril.

"If you guys let me, then I'll sleep on the end next time." Dede was always willing to negotiate.

One night, our new cousin Halle slept over. Halle was Carolina's daughter and Carolina became Auntie Carolina after a decade of dating Uncle Davy. Halle's birthday was between my May and Denise's December. Instead of five fighting over blankets, it was six.

"Stop!" Nancy scolded us then she got up.

We thought she was going to tell Nana, but she stayed in the room and sat on Nana's couch.

"You can't sleep there, Nancy," Dede told her.

"I know."

Nancy appeared to be thinking very hard. Then she stood up and walked to Nana's two stuffed chairs. She pushed them together. The five of us sat up with our mouths open while we watched her and no adults were around to warn us about catching flies. When she was finished and the chairs were facing each other perfectly, she snuggled into her creation with a smile almost as bright as the streetlamp outside the window.

"Please, Nancy, let me sleep with you!" Denise wasn't ashamed to beg first.

"I'm your *sister*, Nance," Dede talked back to Nancy the most, but she took her chances anyway.

"I'm your *cousin*," Marlene tried to wedge herself between Dede and Denise..

"*I'm* your cousin too," I pleaded. Marlene talked back to Nancy the second most and wasn't likely to be chosen.

"I'm skinny and won't take up that much room," Halle said looking at my big panza.

"Nope, I'm sleeping alone," Nancy told us reaching for an itchy, Army blanket from our pile.

Dede pulled it out of reach.

"Yay!" we cheered for Dede.

"That's ok. I don't need it," Nancy said and turned away from us. "Now be quiet and go to sleep or I'll call Nana. And you big girls let the little ones sleep in the middle."

"You can't tell us who sleeps in the middle if you're not sleeping with us," Dede responded.

"Yes, I can. You and Marlene go to the ends. Now."

They waited a short while then moved to an end.

"And, Halle, you go in the middle."

Me and Denise moved on the side of Halle that was next to the other's sister.

"Let's play Tickle," Denise suggested in a whisper.

"She said she's going to tell if we make noise," Halle reminded Denise.

"Go to sleep," Nancy said without turning around.

Denise pulled Halle's chin so she could whisper in her ear. She explained that Tickle was when one of us wrote or drew pictures with our fingers on the back of the one in front of us. Whoever was being drawn on guessed the picture or word on her back then it was the first artist's turn. There was just enough light from outside to do a silent One Potato-Two Potato to figure out who would get their backs tickled first. I lifted the back of my shirt and waited. I felt a finger slide across my back. It started at the top then down, a loop, then up again and down, ending with another loop. Then a lot of little, side drawings that I had no idea what they were, but they felt so good.

"Ok, guess."

"A butterfly?"

"No."

"A car?"

"Nope."

"String?'

"What? You're not even trying to guess."

"I am. It's just...hard. Do it again."

"No. Do me. It's my turn."

"No, I didn't guess right."

"It was my name."

"What?"

"In handwriting."

"I don't know how to handwrite."

"Too bad. My turn." And with that, Dede patted my back to signal she was done and turned and lifted the back of her shirt.

I began my favorite drawing, a house with a face on it. Before I had drawn the chimney, she was snoring.

Out With the Family

"BOO!"

Nana and I jumped in our seats even though we'd heard someone stomping down the hall.

"Want some chow mein?" Uncle Manny asked with an easy smile, holding up a clear, plastic bag with white, Styrofoam to-go boxes inside. He must have come from Kenny's, his then favorite hangout on South Van Ness near 16th.

"Hi, Ma. How's it goin', ol' grey mare?" Uncle said as he crossed in front of Nana.

"We're fine, Manny. Sit down and watch the movie," Nana told him even though he was already on his way to sitting next to me on the couch.

"How's it goin', Barrel?" Uncle Manny said my childhood nickname like I was still five years old.

"Hi, Uncle."

He caught a glimpse of Burt Lancaster.

"What's Moses doing?" he asked me with a thumb curved at the screen.

"It's Burt Lancaster playing Jim Thorpe," I told him.

"Who?"

"Jim Thorpe, the Native American athlete," I said.

"Oh! Those crackers fucked that Indian over!" he said while nodding his head with closed eyes.

"Don't tell us what happens, Manny," Nana scolded.

"What do you mean don't tell you? Everybody knows those assholes fucked him over and stole his medals," he said looking at me. "You went to college. You know that, don't you, Barrel?"

"Well, I was never in a Native American Studies class, but—"

"So, how ya been?" Before I could answer, he sang, "Roll out the Barrel" then chuckled. "'Member that?" then "Ah shit, how's school?" he asked loudly over the movie as if it weren't even on and we weren't even watching it.

"I graduated."

"She graduated, Manny."

"I know. I was there," he scowled at Nana. "I just thought The Barrel might have gone back to brush up on her shit. What'd you study again? Or, uh, what was your major?" he asked with a professorial tone, eyes wide open and eyebrows cocked high.

"English and History."

"History? And you don't know about Jim Thorpe? I know more than Professor Barrel?" he cackled.

Usually, when he was sober, he didn't say a whole lot. He'd nod hello or hold his hand up to say hi. If he was eating something, he'd point at his plate of food then the kitchen inviting us to help ourselves. When we got ready to go, he'd nod or hold up his hand again. When he was drinking, there was no keeping him quiet.

"Yeah, you know more than I do."

I peeked at Uncle. He was sitting up and staring directly at me with the widest goofy grin, his thin mustache dancing above his upper lip.

"Aw, go to hell!" He waved me off to turn back to the TV and I did too.

Even with Burt Lancaster playing the lead role, Jim Thorpe's story was more interesting than I expected. I didn't know anything about the Carlisle Indian School. Somewhere along the way, I had heard something about Thorpe competing in the Olympics. A commercial for musical hits from the 1950s came on.

"Someone to watch over me..." a voice crooned. I remembered reading those words in a condolence card when Mom passed. One of her high school friends said it had been one of Mom's favorite songs. It is one of those nuggets of information that I still hold onto.

I felt Uncle Manny staring at me.

"Your mother loved that song," he said. He scooted up on the couch and stared at the TV before turning to Nana, "Didn't she, Ma?"

"What?"

"Mono. That song. She liked it."

"I don't know. She liked a lot of music. Frank Sinatra, mariachis, those colored singers."

"Yeah, he's one of those *colored singers*, Ma. Same goddamn color as our black asses." He mumbled something else then turned to me again, "Your mother liked a lot of different music, but I know she really liked him. John-ny...? Mathis! That's who's singing that song. He's from here."

"The City?"

"A-huh." Then he seemed to remember something and chuckled to himself. "Remember the Fickle Fox?"

"No, what's that?"

"You know, uh, Mission Playground?"

"Where Nickel Pool is?"

"Yeah, Nickel Pool, Mission Playground, same thing. You remember Jets that used to be there on Valencia?"

Dozens of clear light bulbs arranged in a one and nine advertising their fries flashed through my mind.

"Yeah."

"Remember across the little street from Jets there was a bar?"

A smiling animal face on a white background appeared in my mind. I'd never noticed it was a fox.

"Yeah, yeah, I remember." I felt happy to share this memory with Uncle. Jets was torn down for the little park's expansion and Fickle Fox was turned into a trendy tapas bar.

"Well, I was walking to Mama's, I mean Nana's, one day and I passed by that damn place. I peeked in and who did I see?"

I had no idea and didn't guess.

"Fucken Johnny Mathis!"

"Cool!" I remembered seeing a faded red and black 45 with his name and "Chances Are" in the stacks of Mom's records. "Did you tell my Mom?"

"Yeah, I told her he was in there." Then he exhaled loudly. "She was uh...disappointed...well uh...surprised. 'Aw, Manny!'" He mimicked her. "It was a bar...for...uhm...gays."

Gay was one word that did not get mentioned in Nana's house. Or any family member's house. OK, it was mentioned but not really. Growing up surrounded by 49ers Faithful and Raiders Haters, the only time I heard anything close to gay was when my uncles watched their cross-bay rivals demolish the homeboys in red and gold on the football field and used both f-words "fuck" and "fag" in all their variations.

One Halloween when Nana still lived across from Mission High, we trick-or-treated from Church to Castro. We raced up 18th ringing buzzers, running up and down stairs. We barged into grocery stores and bars. The bar patrons sprinkled coins and bills into our bags. We reached Castro where there was a huge crowd then our adult relative-escorts quickly ushered us back down 18th. Before they turned us back, I saw a man in a dress. I recognized something about myself in him. That Halloween and the special twinges I felt for certain girls that had been happening since before I started kindergarten scared me. Or my family's reaction. Or both.

Nana glanced at Uncle Manny then Jim. I concentrated on Jim.

"Did you know it was a gay bar?" he asked me.

I paused. I didn't want to answer his question. *What would he ask next,* I wondered.

"Nah, I had no idea."

"Quiet, Manny, we're trying to watch the movie," Nana tried to nudge him to silence.

"I'm just trying to talk to my niece, Ma."

I was ready to be quiet for the rest of the night.

"Hey, I ran into Auntie Daisy earlier tonight at the Dovre Club," he announced.

Auntie Daisy had asked me to stay with Nana so she could have a few hours out. Nana and Uncle Manny lived with Auntie. Last year before they moved in, I showed up on Auntie's doorstep with tears and mocos running down my face. She brought me in and through heaving and hic-cupping, I told her about my love since high school for a friend. She shhh-shhhd until I fell asleep on her couch. She had always been open and kind-hearted and after that night she became more so. Alone or with friends, I'd visit her at her place or a nearby family favorite pub. I asked her not to tell anyone and she promised not to.

"She told me you're going to be selling sodas tomorrow."

"Mm-hm," I pretended to focus on the movie.

"What's the group raising the money for?"

"A retreat," I answered truthfully but not completely.

"You all go off in the woods or some shit like that?"

I'd never been on a retreat—let alone a lesbian retreat—and was kind of unsure myself. I felt anxious that Auntie must have told him my secret.

"I guess whatever everybody decides they want to do."

Please, God, make him pass out.

"Just women in the woods?"

Then I knew he knew.

"You have to go to work in a few hours," Nana said. "Why don't you go to bed so we can watch this movie in peace?"

"Aw, fuck work. Barrel'll call me in. Won't you?"

I'd heard him ask Nana, Auntie Maggie, Auntie Daisy, and some of my cousins to call into work for him. I didn't feel like doing him any favors right then, but I couldn't say no. We weren't raised to say no to our elders. They said Go to the store, we jumped up and went. They said go back, we ran back.

Jim caught the ball and ran past defender after defender. I wished I was Jim, running and running. I'd run out the livingroom, down the stairs, to the top of Guerrero, down 23rd to my flat on Alabama. I eyed Nana. She was watching Jim.

"It's a lesbian group, Ma. They're gonna sell sodas at the Gay Parade for their lesbian retreat," Uncle Manny said casually as if he were announcing a Giants' score then sank back into the couch letting his head droop down to his chest.

I stopped breathing. My eyes widened. I tried to blink them back to normal size. My eyelashes were the only things moving. Nana sat frozen for at least a full minute. The announcer announced that we would take a break for their sponsors before returning with the final scenes.

I couldn't turn to Nana, but I imagined that she was wishing she could run away too. Finally, she scooted up in her seat and very carefully removed her glasses. She folded them and put them in her flowery, cushioned pouch. She picked up each puzzle book and folded each cover back to the front. She picked up her pill containers from the side table. She put everything in her bag that hung across the front bar of her walker.

Uncle lifted his head, snorted "She's a lesbian, Ma," then his head plopped down again.

Nana adjusted her bag then sat on the edge of her chair. Uncle Manny tilted his head back against the couch and exhaled as if he was exhausted.

"Ah, what the fuck? It's your own damn business, your own damn business," he mumbled more to himself than to me.

Jim returned. Nana and I watched him throw a football to a group of young boys. "THE END" plastered over Jim's body before the screen faded. A cubic zirconium commercial came on then one for a little machine that diced, sliced, and chopped carrots. Nana turned to me.

"Are you staying the night?"

"No." I didn't usually and for sure wasn't going to that night.

"He's here," she pointed at Uncle with her long, brown finger.

"I'll go when Auntie gets back."

"She comes in late."

"I'm ok waiting." I might have left if I thought my legs could carry me.

"You don't have to wait for her."

"I'll watch some more TV," she knew I didn't have a TV at my place.

"You have your car?"

"Mm-hm."

"Well, you know where the blankets are if you decide to stay or wanna lay down."

"Ah-huh, yeah."

"Okay. Be careful if you go home tonight."

"Okay, Nana, good night," I said a little too fast. I didn't raise my head, but once she turned away from me I started breathing again.

From the corner of my eyes, I saw her stop in front of Uncle.

"Manny, get some sleep before you have to get up for work in a few hours."

He didn't respond. I was relieved that he had passed out. She dismissed him with a wave of her hand and pushed her walker out the door.

"Did the ol' grey mare leave?" he asked as soon as he heard her rolling down the hallway.

I turned and saw he had one eye open, "Yes, she left."

"Whatever the hell you do," he said with his index finger bobbing, "don't ever" bob-bob-bob "act like" bob-bob "your shit don't stink" bob-bob-bob-bob.

I knew this was his worst insult.

"Okay, Uncle, I won't," I promised.

He viewed me with dissatisfaction.

"I won't act like...My...Shit...Doesn't stink."

He nodded.

"There's this asshole who comes to the bar and he always acts like his fucken shit don't stink. I hate him and it don't got nothin' to do with him being" his fingers waved "that way. Like you."

Uncle Manny busted me out to Nana then said he knew—drank with—a gay man. This was my chance to ask him about Jim Plunkett.

"Okay, I'll try not to. I won't...Uncle?"

"What?"

"Uh, how'd you know Jim Plunkett is gay?"

"What? Shut the fuck up! I'm going to bed. Call my damn job. The number's on the wall. Tell them I might be fifteen minutes late, but I'm coming in."

"Ok."

"And get twenty bucks outta my wallet for a cab for when you go home," he said as he pulled his wallet from his right back pocket and flung it on the couch.

"Thanks, Uncle, but I have my car."

"What'd I tell ya? Don't act like your shit don't stink. Take the damn twenty," he pointed at his wallet.

"But I have—"

"Take it for gas money then, goddammit."

"Ok, thanks."

"Damn kids think they know everything. Didn't even know who the fuck Jim Thorpe was. Brings up that asshole Plunkett."

He mumbled a few more things as he walked down the hall to his bedroom. He pushed the door open and banged it close. I heard the springs from him falling on his bed and then nothing.

I called the Hostess office and passed on his message. I channel-surfed for a couple of minutes, but nothing caught my interest. I kept thinking about what it would be like the next time I saw Nana and the rest of the family. Tonight wasn't great, but it was better than some scenes I had imagined. I understood about Auntie Daisy not keeping my secret, but I couldn't face her yet. I wasn't angry. I was kind of relieved that I had told her, she told Uncle, and he told Nana. I wouldn't have ever been able to do that.

I walked to the porch and twisted the back door knob. I came back into the kitchen and turned the burners. I made sure the remote was on top of the TV then I turned off all the lights except one. Finally, I reached for Uncle's wallet and dragged out a twenty and slid it inside mine. Then I left it in the middle of the kitchen table.

I put on my jacket and strapped my backpack over my right shoulder. I walked downstairs, opened the door, and felt the crisp City air. Cars zipped up and over Guerrero. I clicked the door handle, locked it in place, and pulled it shut. I stood and watched the traffic light go through its color drill. The streetlamp overhead beamed bright then burned out. I stepped off and went hunting for my Chevette.

I Say A Little Prayer for You

"Ramona, do you know where you are?"

"No," she answered tiredly. I started to laugh. Nana looked at me. I stopped. I was an 18-year old freshman at San Francisco State and Nana still scared me.

"Do you know today's date?" as he rolled from her left side to right on a small stool, the doctor shined a light and peered into Mom's eyes.

"No," she sighed.

"Do you know who the president is?"

Say Tuesday. Say stupid Reagan's name. Come on, Mom. Quit playing around. Cómo friegas!

We weren't supposed to say "Cómo friegas." It was so annoying how Mom didn't teach us Spanish then the things we heard we couldn't even say. Or, we couldn't say to her. She said "Cómo friegas" all the time to us. My sister said it once when we were boarding the 14, right there on the corner of 24th and Mission. Back when we were kids and it was just a corner.

That day getting on the bus, we had been in and out of the little mom and pop shops on Mission and Mom's favorites, the big department stores on Market Street—The Emporium, Macy's, Liberty House, I. Magnin, Joseph Magnin. We each hugged the bags in our arms and gripped the coin in our hands. As she was stepping up, Marlene tripped and dropped all her bags and nickel right there in front of the driver and the other families going home. "Cómo friegas!" Marlene belted loud and clear. Everybody on the bus started laughing.

"Quiet!!!" Mom hushed us like if Marlene had said the f-word.

Mom's eyes widened and her nose and mouth were scrunched up in a ball. She looked like she did the day she gave us the worst spanking of our lives. I looked away from Mom and made the mistake of looking at Marlene who was holding onto the fare box to steady her. Her bags were still on the floor. I started laughing again.

"You too!" Mom yelled pointing at me.

Then the people on the bus started laughing again.

In that room with the flickering light, I stood there wondering why Mom wasn't answering the questions and why that doctor wasn't giving her a shot or some pills to make her better. I wanted to say "Cómo friegas!" to him. I looked at Nana and kept my mouth shut.

"Ramona, listen to me very carefully. Do you know who the president is?"

"Ah-uh," Mom muttered as her chin dropped and her eyes closed.

"She's a sick girl, doctor," Nana said.

"Yes, she is. I'm admitting her.

Me and Nana visited Mom the next morning. Mom knew where she was.

"Hi, Mija. Hi, Ma."

"Mom! You scared me," I said walking towards her.

"I know. I'm sorry," she said looking a little embarrassed as she hugged me.

"How you feeling, Mono?"

"I'm ok, Ma."

A new doctor came in.

"I'm Ramona's primary doctor. I've ordered a bunch of tests for her."

"What's wrong with her, doctor?" Nana asked.

"I don't know. She might have some kind of infection. I've told Ramona that we're in the preliminary stages of coming up with a diagnosis. It might be some kind of cancer."

"Cancer?" I blurted out.

"Yes, possibly. You should know it might even be AIDS."

AIDS pushed cancer from my mind. I was in love with my friend from high school, but I wanted nothing to do with AIDS. It had been talked about as the "gay cancer." Then it crawled up the social ladder to a sexually transmitted disease or a disease contracted by IV drug users. I felt very scared and very ashamed. I blamed Mom for being sick. If she hadn't been messing around with that married man she wouldn't be here, I thought.

Before examining Mom, taking her temperature and blood pressure, or bringing in her food, Dr. Stuart and the nurses pulled on gloves and masks and gowns. They told us to do the same. Each time I slipped my arms through the gown or tied the mask over my face, I felt like I was pushing Mom away. Each time I rolled on a pair of gloves, I felt like I was betraying her. She couldn't understand any of us through masks. It was hard to breathe through them. The gowns kept falling off. After a couple days, only the medical staff wore the protective gear.

Everyday there were so many of us sitting in the room with Mom, standing outside in the hall, and walking to and from the cafeteria. Me, Nana, Marlene, Ray, and Frank usually came first thing in the morning. The aunties and uncles came by after work. My cousins visited as often as they could. Other family we hadn't seen in years or had never met started to drop in throughout the days and evenings.

The blood and urine tests, CAT scans, and spinal taps weren't enough to give the doctors an idea of how to treat her. I understood what they were saying, but I didn't believe them. I didn't believe I was going to a hospital everyday instead of school. I missed a week of classes before I withdrew from State. I sold my books and told myself that I would re-enroll in the fall when everything was back to normal.

Mom missed a week of work. She never missed a whole week of work. She didn't take vacations. Maybe a weekend trip to Nevada where she played the penny slots. Occasionally, Mom took one or two vacation days when one of us kids was sick. Sometimes when she was tired. Years of dancing all night at The Crossroads with her girlfriends who were in their 20s caught up with her when she hit 40. Sometimes she stayed home after a long night or nights of playing hang-up-the-phone on that boyfriend. Most of the time, she was tired from a weekend of cooking or cleaning up after our birthday parties or extra big family get-togethers. Sometimes, she just didn't feel like putting on what she called her work uniform: skirt, blouse, sensible pumps.

I liked going to the cafeteria with relatives and talking over tuna sandwiches or cheap grilled burgers. I liked them asking me how I was doing and listening to me. I felt bad for liking the fun times at the hospital. I told myself I shouldn't be enjoying this time and if I did I would get punished. Something might really happen to Mom. I told myself that was silly. I knew I really wanted her home with me more than a relative buying me a hot chocolate.

By the second week, Mom's skin turned yellow. Her cheekbones were starting to be noticeable. The doctors stressed the need for us to allow more tests to try to determine the cause of Mom's illness.

"Her liver is worsening," Dr. Stuart told us. "How's her drinking? Does she drink?"

She drank every weekend. OK, not every weekend. Most weekends. Three weekends out of four. Friday or Saturday night but not both. Unless it was a special occasion like a holiday, birthday, extra hard work week. As Alicia Bridges would sing, Mom was a lady who "loved the night life, loved to boogie on the disco 'round." Yes, she liked to drink, but really she just wanted to dance. She was very clear: she went to clubs to dance. Mom was the family dancer. When there was a Soul Train line, she was the one who had started it. I knew the doctor wouldn't understand.

"She drinks."

"A lot? A little? Is she a social drinker?"

"Yeah, she's a social drinker."

"What about smoking. Does she smoke?"

Just when she was out drinking. She didn't smoke at home. Unless she was mad at that boyfriend. This was usually after screaming on the phone to him. Then she'd go to the store herself and buy a pack of Kool Milds, a pint of Seagram's, and a can of 7-Up. She'd close the livingroom door before playing Aretha's haunting ballads, Bobby "The Poet" Womack growling about the hard times, or Jerry "The Iceman" Butler coolly describing devastating love. The livingroom shelves were full of stacks of 45s and LP spines, but there were only a few who she pulled to keep her company in the dark. Whiffs of smoke and the red light from the stereo escaped through the keyhole. If they weren't fighting, that boyfriend would bring over a bottle of white wine and they'd finish it sitting together on the couch. No cigarettes.

"Social smoker."

Dr. Stuart told us about billirubin, a measurement of a liver's health. He said a normal liver was at one and Mom's was at eighteen. Her skin turned yellow. She lost her appetite. Twice she bled. Dr. Stuart ordered a transfusion of platelets. He had told us when she was first brought in that bleeding wouldn't be a good sign.

This was hard news for everyone. All the news that came our way was hard. It was also confusing. Every day, Dr. Stuart or an on-duty resident came by and updated Mom and whoever was in the room on her condition. There were not only medical terms to understand, but they needed permission for the tests. Someone needed to communicate on a regular basis with the nurses. We all tried to keep track of Mom's medication. Too soon after Mom was admitted, Dr. Stuart started talking about what ifs and after.

Then an aunt (by a very recent marriage) said she didn't think the doctors were doing all they could and she was going to transfer Mom to another hospital. This aunt's threats unified us four kids. At 18, 19, 22, and 23 years old, we decided that we would be the go-to people. We gathered our courage to tell Nana that we would meet with the doctors every day at 5 o'clock for the day's briefing then pass the information to her and the rest of the family.

By the third week, the doctors told us we should start thinking about "afterwards." I didn't want to. I was afraid that anything less than one hundred percent faith might cause it to happen. I believed we had to stay positive and keep encouraging Mom to get better. Dr. Stuart kept asking if we were going to move Mom to another hospital. What did we want to do about life support machines? Would we approve an autopsy? He told us to continue to tend to her affairs. I went to Mom's job and got her check then cashed it and paid the rent when she was living at the hospital. I felt awful, but I told myself I did it so she would have a place to come home to. I was trying to be hopeful and he kept sounding like she wasn't coming home.

Then Dr. Stuart said we should appoint one of us four to be the executor of her estate. I didn't tell him that the converted garage we were living in wasn't an estate. He started asking, Which of you will tell her about her condition? If the time comes, do you want the nurses to help or not? We'll take care of her, we said. We rotated staying by Mom's side.

One night, Auntie Ellie asked me to stay at her house. I didn't want to leave Mom, but Auntie said I could help Mom more if I rested. That night, Marlene stayed by Mom's side. Auntie drove me to Pacifica, made me a good dinner and let me sleep late. When she brought me back to the hospital the next day, Marlene told me that Mom kept calling for me during the night.

"What'd she want to tell me? What'd I miss?"

Marlene didn't know and I still wonder.

Dad came to visit Mom and brought yellow roses. I'd always been glad they had divorced because I couldn't imagine them together. By the time I started kindergarten, he had taken the boys and was gone. Dad moved back to suburbia and dated White women. He remarried two years after the divorce. She was a great stepmom and I told her.

Mom and Dad had lived in the suburbs for most of their marriage. When they divorced, they were back in the City where they had met. She stayed in the City and dated Black men. She moved us to the Haight to live with her first boyfriend Mel. He was funny and kind with Marlene and me, but he broke Mom's heart. After that, she moved us in with Nana and Grandpa. She never remarried, never lived outside the City again.

I knew I was so lucky for having no memories of the fights Mom and Dad must have had. I have only a few, fuzzy memories of us all together. I always told myself, fuzzy's better than bad. I just knew that if they had stayed together, their arguments would've been worse than Mom had with that last boyfriend.

As corny as it sounds when I saw Dad patting Mom's hand, I didn't want him to stop. And I wanted him to stay and help us bring Mom home. Dad came out of the room and called us four over.

"How's Mom? What'd she say?" Frank asked.

"Your mother doesn't want another spinal tap."

"She didn't tell us that," Frank said looking at us three.

"She told me. No more."

"The doctors need to do them," Ray said.

"Yeah, Dad, Dr. Stuart said they need to do it to find out--" Marlene tried.

"No. They hurt her."

"They have to hurt her to help her," I said.

"No. And if the time comes, she doesn't want an autopsy."

"Dad, how are we going to know what made her sick?" I didn't want Mom to go, but I wanted to know what was taking her.

"Your mother said no."

That was the only time I heard Dad speak about Mom as if they had ever seen each other as anyone other than "your mother" or "your father." Then he went home to my stepmother. I had given my stepmother Mother's Day cards for years and would again, but at that moment I wished my Mom had her husband.

"Take things day-by-day," Dr. Stuart said. "It's useless to let your moods fluctuate based on her daily bilirubin count."

All we have is her daily bilirubin count, I wanted to tell him. Mom's bilirubin went to 26. He said Mom had about two or three more weeks but not to hold him to that. He said she might lapse into a coma if the bilirubin reached 40, but it could happen at 30.

Nana said she wanted to talk to us. We found an empty lounge in the hospital away from the crowd of relatives.

"Your mother's tired. She's a very sick woman," she said looking around at each of us four. "Yous kids need to tell her that you'll be fine." Then with her head slightly bent but looking up into my eyes, she added, "Yous need to tell her to go in peace."

Are you crazy, old lady? I couldn't believe Nana. *What are you thinking? I won't be fine. I need her.* When we left the lounge and went back to the room, I didn't tell Mom anything about me being ok without her.

The day after Nana's talk, I was holding Mom's hand, rubbing it. Then she held my hand and brought it to her lips and kissed it. It felt like years since Mom had kissed me. It wasn't. She had given me kisses in the hospital, but this kiss felt different. All the hospital kisses were different. I didn't know when the next one would come or if there'd be a next one. Then she released my hand.

"Catherine, that plant. It was flying."

I laughed hearing what she said but not understanding while she pointed limply to an area between the dresser and window. I looked where she directed. I knew what she was saying, but I didn't know why. She sensed my confusion.

"It flew, mija. It did."

I wanted to believe her. I tried very hard to imagine how the plant could have flown. The only scenario I could come up with was space aliens coming in and carrying the plant back and forth. I felt bad for laughing at Mom. I felt bad for every time I was away from her side. I was sorry for blaming her for being sick. Sorry for judging her. Sorry for being embarrassed about being evicted. Sorry for having fallen in love with that girl. With any girl. I was sorry for talking back, not washing dishes, not making my bed, not putting my clothes away, not starting dinner, not dancing with her.

By the fourth week, Dr. Stuart said Mom had an eighty percent chance of survival. He said exploratory surgery was their best and last chance to find out what was wrong with her so they could treat her effectively. The four of us gave our permission. Before they finished prepping her, the surgeons cancelled the procedure.

One time when we were living on Guerrero, Mom had a sore on her back. It just appeared and grew bigger and redder over a couple of days. Finally, she went next door to Nana's flat. I followed. Mom found Nana in the kitchen where she usually was and told her about the sore. Nana finished washing dishes while she listened to Mom. Nana asked Mom a few questions then dried her hands.

"Let's see," Nana said. "Go ahead, sit down." Nana pointed with her chin at one of the chairs with curlicue black wrought iron-looking backs. Mom sat down. Nana lifted her blouse.
"I'll be right back, Mono."

Nana went to get a bath towel then returned.

"Take off your shirt."

Mom unbuttoned her blouse and slipped it off. Nana handed the towel to her and Mom covered her breasts with it.

"Lean over."

Mom leaned over Nana's kitchen table. Nana pulled her black, cat eyeglasses from her apron pocket and placed her index and middle fingers near Mom's sore. She massaged deep into Mom's back. I had never seen Nana touch Mom on purpose except for New Year's Eve hugs. Maybe they squeezed by one another trying to get from one room to another when there was a bunch of people in the flat but nothing like this.

"I have to get something," Nana said heading to the porch.

I heard clicking sounds then the back door opened. Nana went out then returned with a small branch from one of the sad trees. She set the branch in the dish drain. She pulled one of her pots from the pantry and filled it with water then set it on the front burner with a high flame. She pulled leaves off the branch and placed them in the pot. She covered the pot. Once the water boiled, she turned off the flame.

"Ok, this is going to be a little hot."

Nana put a pot holder on the table in front of Mom. She lifted the lid and put it in the sink. Then she removed each leaf and laid them on Mom's back. She massaged around Mom's sore again then lifted the leaves. A two-inch long thorn emerged from the wound. Nana pulled it all the way out.

"Put your shirt back on," Nana said patting Mom's shoulder. After she did, Nana gathered the thorn, all the leaves, the branch, and the towel and went back outside. She came back in and lit a Marlboro. Mom's back never bothered her again.

I went to Mom. I found her hand underneath the sheet and held it. She didn't respond. I touched her gray hair that was taking over the auburn-brown magic from a L'Oreal 'cause-she-was-worth-it box. I placed my hand on her yellowed cheek, her yellowed forehead. Her skin sagged on her bones. She hadn't been fat or heavy, but she had had some "extra meat on her bones" as she liked to say. Her freckles were faded. I blew on her hairline. The first time I did that as a child, she laughed and told me to stop. She said Dad used to do that to her. I blew again and again. Her lips didn't part, her gap tooth smile didn't appear.

"I'm sorry, Mom."

Her only movements were her eyes flitting involuntarily beneath their lids.

"It's okay, Mom. Don't worry about me."

You know I don't mean this, right Mom?

"I'll be ok. You can go."

Really, Mom, I want you to stay with me. We'll find a place on Chenery. Remember we were walking around one day and found that street? It's close to State and right on a couple of bus lines. There's even a BART station nearby. You can catch it to work and get off at Civic Center. I'll finish school then move us to Oakland, San Jose, anywhere. I'll get us a house and you can play Stevie, Diana, Teddy, and Marvin on Saturday mornings as loud as you want. I won't even complain when you throw on Toña la Negra or Amalia Mendoza. You can sit in the backyard with your big, tortoise shell sunglasses covering half your face and pretend you can hear the congas in Dolores Park. You can dance all over the patio. I'll dance with you. You won't even have to ask me. The family can come over and make tamales on New Year's Eve. You can retire. I'll be a teacher and have summers off. I'll take you on real vacations to Hawaii or Mexico. We'll stay for a week, two weeks. We can do it, Mom. We'll do it. Come on, Mom, let's go home.

Burn the Mission

i want to
evict every café
pile every cell phone
on top of
million dollar lofts
pour gas
throw match
fan flames

wait for the air to clear
and breathe
again

Dot Com Boom

speculators flipped homes like hotcakes
buildings burnt down
causes "unknown"
but you knew
millions of dollars going up

We organized
Homes Yes!
Evictions No!

We marched
¡Hogares sí!
¡Desarrollos no!

Developers hired Irish
who subcontracted Black and Latino
who tore down our city
then built it back up
without leaving space for us
or themselves

We
elders artists immigrants queers youth
parents students activists
packed City Hall chambers
for planning commission meetings

the hammers and chisels
hovered over us

suits slipped into offices
left gifts for un-supervised
supervisors and mayor
who couldn't see past their bank accounts

We the public
waited hours to be summoned
to deliver our comments
for the allotted two whole minutes

Joshua's testimony ticked past 120 seconds
       president warned
             bailiff stepped
"Please, your Honor"
       president warned
             toward Joshua
"Your honor, we need more time"
       president warned
             next to Joshua
Joshua kept testifying
       president nodded
             bailiff swung Joshua's arm to chandelier
             slammed Joshua's face into floor

We rose up
president called a recess
called the cops
evicted us for disorderly conduct

planning commission approved
every proposal in the pipeline

we returned to all we had
the streets

¡Hogares sí!
¡Desarrollos no!

Homes Yes!
Evictions No!

Arellano

Salvation on Mission Street

"You should turn back now," Angel told me. That was hours ago. We said we were waiting for a 14 to take her home, but when a bus came we kept saying, "Next one."

I didn't feel the cold and I didn't hear the men's "Oye, mijas" when we passed Hunt's Donuts Open 25 Hours with my arm around Angel. I'd walked on Mission to and from 24th Street so many times before, but that evening the sky had the richest pinks, oranges, and purples mixing with the blue. The palm trees looked perfect standing in the small patches of dirt surrounded by the red and blue bricks of the Mission Miracle Mile. Two weeks ago, the Niners beat the Cowboys in the NFC game. It was a whole new world.

At 24th and Mission, home to the 49ers Faithful and site of The First International Cruise Night, there were more people in the nearby mural than on the street. The viejos on the corner had carried off their card table and bottles of secret waters. The Cristiano strapped his Mr. Microphone to his back after he gave out his last flyer. Horace Mann Middle School and St. Peter's kids had bought paletas then chased each other home hours ago. The Asian woman who was selling the hammer and sickle newspaper— the one that no one in my family ever bought—packed up when the sun first started setting.

I felt like I was on a movie set. It was so quiet and empty. Just Angel and me. With my arm around her. It was cold and we were trying to keep warm, I told myself as I prayed we could stay in that spot for the rest of my life. Mom was probably home from work wondering where I was. Or, she was having a Seven-7 at the Crossroads and not thinking about me. Either way, I wasn't leaving Angel.

"Jesus loves you."

Angel and I let go of each other and looked around. The tall, slender woman with light brown hair and light eyes reminded me of that well-meaning 4th grade teacher who told me I wasn't like the others.

"Jesus loves you," the woman told us smiling and holding a Bible.

Angel smiled back at the woman. I maddogged her.

"Yes, he loves you," she said looking back and forth at us. My wannabe maddogging didn't make her stop.

Angel and I looked at each other then back at the woman. We giggled.

"Haven't you ever heard that at your church?" she asked.

The adults only went to church for the occasional baptism, communion, or wedding. While us kids were at Mission Dolores on Saturdays for catechism classes and Sundays for mass, the uncles went to their own place of worship: in front of the TV on Saturdays for Giants games and Sundays for 49ers. When we came home, there was a game on and we learned the basics of each sport while we traded empties for cold ones. Most of the priests at Mission Dolores were like our uncles and talked about what we did wrong not about Jesus loving us.

"He loved you so much, He died for you," the lady said. "Won't you love Him back and accept Him into your hearts?"

Angel didn't go to church. Her mama lit candles, broke eggs, and left glasses of water around. Her mama bought weed and soaked it in alcohol to cure Angel and her little brothers and sisters when they were sick.

"I wish my Mom would rub weed on me," I told Angel when she first shared her secret with me.

Angel stepped closer to the woman. If I had been with Estrella, Gloria, Ana, or even Andrea we would've just walked away from that loca with the Bible and gone to fired up.

The lady remained between Angel and me. She told us stories about Jesus, some that sounded vaguely familiar and others I just knew she was making up. After she talked to us for half the night, she looked at Angel on her left and me on her right.

"Won't you accept the Lord?"

I wondered to myself, *Am I still buzzed?* Angel looked at me then at the lady.

"I accept the Lord," she said.

I wasn't buzzed. I was with Angel.

There on 24th standing next to Angel and hearing that lady talk, my Jesus, the beautiful blonde-haired blue-eyed Joe Montana, appeared to me.

The lady turned my way, "Do *you* take the Lord Jesus Christ to be *your* savior?"

I looked past the lady and directly at Angel just as two weeks earlier Montana must have locked eyes with Freddie Stuart, Lenvil Elliott, Earl Cooper, and Dwight Clark before each pass or hand off.

The lady stepped closer to me, "Say it. Say, 'I accept the Lord Jesus Christ to be my savior.'"

The streetlight hit Angel as she peered at me with glossy eyes matching her lips as she gripped her books in front of her breasts. Maybe it was the Olde English from earlier. Maybe it was the weed from the day before. All I know is I heard

"Do you—"

I became Dwight Clark rolling into the end zone, turning inside, and stopping between those two defenders. I saw Joe being chased to the right then throwing. I broke for the outside. Then there was only one guy on me.

"Do...you...take..."

I leaped into the air as high as I could. I extended my arms, hands.

"Do you take Angel to be your lawfully wedded wife?"

"I do," I said. And I meant it so help me God. My fingers clutched that ball as if it were my life. I leaned over and kissed Angel. Right there in the Center of the Universe, Angel kissed me back.

"Stop! What are you doing?" the lady tried to pull us apart, but I stiff-armed her.

The crowd cheered. It was a madhouse.

Fly Away

In February of 1995, after two weeks, the doctors of St. Luke's Hospital still couldn't explain why Auntie Daisy was sick. They performed numerous tests, but they had no diagnosis. With Auntie Daisy rapidly losing weight and the doctors unable to find a cause, I tried not to remember what had happened with Mom years earlier.

Nancy and Denise, two of Auntie Daisy's daughters living in Southern California, flew up to be with their mother. They visited Auntie Daisy, discussed her status with the doctors, and made sure Markie, Jessie, Kyle, and Uncle Manny were doing fine without her. When Auntie Daisy's health stabilized but before she was released, Nancy and Denise returned to their homes. Auntie Daisy came home a few weeks later, and Nancy and Denise flew up for a long weekend to check up on their mother.

"Let's get together before you go home," I called and asked them.

It was kind of silly to call and ask. Everyone in the family was going to Auntie Daisy's house almost every day even before she went into the hospital. Her house had become the headquarters of family life like Nana's house when I was growing up. Those of us who lived with Auntie Daisy and those of us who visited every day just tried to be more useful when she was released.

"Sure, sure. My Mom says meet us at Jim's," Nancy said, directing me to Auntie Daisy's favorite diner on Mission Street. I hung up then worked on some poems for an upcoming reading. When I was done, I remembered I already had a date with my new girlfriend Vero. I knew it'd be ok if I brought her, but I called Auntie's house one more time. If we were still meeting at Jim's, we'd need an extra seat.

Too much time passed before there was a "Hello."

"Oh, hey, Nancy. If we're really meeting at Jim's then-"

"Cath, you better come over," Nancy told me. I knew then that I didn't want to go over. I could hear it in her voice. All the way walking from my place on 23rd and Alabama to Auntie Daisy's flat on 19th and Guerrero, I did my best to pray without praying. I didn't want God to punish anyone for my sudden faithfulness.

It's not Nana. It can't be Nana. Auntie Daisy has been feeling well. Maybe... please not Auntie Daisy. I didn't hear anything in Nancy's voice, right? Please let me be wrong.

I arrived at the flat, pushed open the unlocked door, and walked up the stairs. Nancy met me at the top of the landing, "It's Uncle."

"What?"

"He had a cold and went to bed last night. We heard him get up for a bowl of cereal. He went back to his room, coughed, then he was quiet."

He slipped away from us. I had wondered about Uncle Manny. I knew that Auntie Daisy was planning to move to Southern California to be near her kids and grandkids. Because they were so close, I worried how Uncle would manage without her. I knew his daughters lived in the Bay and son was in Nevada. He had his buddy Uncle Sammy, but Auntie Daisy looked after him. Uncle Manny and Auntie Daisy were very happy living together with her young adult children Markie, Jessie, and Jessie's son.

I had been looking forward to Uncle Manny meeting Vero and saying something funny to make her laugh. Instead the night before his funeral, Vero met my family for the first time. We laughed a lot listening and telling stories about Uncle Manny, but we wanted him not stories.

Nancy and Denise stayed another few days. Because of Auntie Daisy's illness and Uncle Manny's passing, this was the most I had seen them in years and it felt good even though circumstances were hard.

"Man, you guys," Denise told us gathered at Auntie Daisy's flat one evening before they left. "I couldn't live in this city again. I don't miss anything about this dang place. I like Southern California with its warm weather, good malls, and cheaper rent. But I wish you all lived down there too."

I wished that we lived near each other again too. But up north.

A few years earlier, Nancy and I had been talking on the phone. I asked her if she ever thought about moving home. She said it crossed her mind briefly but never for long. She loved her two sons and watching them grow up. She had a good job and her and her husband had bought a house with a big yard. A corner lot for the boys to play, she proudly told me. Throughout her visit, she was passing around photos of the boys and telling stories about their sweet and naughty adventures. The hardest part about coming up to help Auntie Daisy was being away from them.

In early summer, a bunch of us were at Auntie Daisy's watching the Giants lose to the Dodgers for the millionth time.

"I have some news," she announced during commercial.

"What?" Dinky asked for all of us.

"Nancy's pregnant!"

"All right!" Stephie exclaimed.

We toasted to Nancy and her baby's health. We knew that she'd been wanting another baby. She had enjoyed helping Jessie playing with, feeding, and dressing Kyle when she had been up in March. In October when Nancy went to the hospital, Auntie Daisy told us there were complications. The baby was fine but Nancy wasn't. Auntie Maggie helped Auntie Daisy get a quick flight south. Carloads of us--aunts, uncles, and cousins--drove down and crowded with her in-laws in the waiting room and Nancy's house waiting for her to recover. After a few days when her health somewhat stabilized, us Northern Cal family came home. Except Auntie Daisy and Nancy's siblings.

The call came one night after I'd been fighting with Vero. Marlene told me what I didn't want to hear in words that I can't remember. The argument ended and Vero held me.

My Pendleton, My Love

"Shao!"

It was Friday morning before school, and I was checking out myself in the bathroom mirror. I was wearing my new favorite outfit: creased navy blue Ben's, no-creased-but-starched flat white t-shirt, black canvas winos, carefully folded and ironed-after-each-fold blue handkerchief hanging from my back pocket. Last and most importantly, I was wearing the Pendleton my brother Ray had given me. It was a Pendleton. It didn't *look* like a Pendleton. It didn't *feel* like a Pendleton. It *was* a Pendleton. A real, live Pendleton on wannabe me.

Not only was it a Pendleton, but it was the sweetest shade of baby blue with a hint of grey that added a touch of class. I'm horrible with fashion. Ask my sister who stopped me from wearing bright red socks to third grade one day and I still don't know why. But even I could appreciate this work of art.

"That's coooool!" I said when I saw Ray wearing it for the first time on a visit to my Dad's house.

He saw my love for his Pendleton and when he asked, "Do you want-"

"Yes!" I answered. Just as I did ten years later when he asked me to babysit his clean Monte Carlo lowriding machine before the Army gave him a year-long all-expenses paid trip to South Korea.

As quickly as I could, I peeled my Pendleton off my brother and slipped it on my body. The cuffs needed to be folded a few times but I didn't care. All us kids wore baggy clothes. I knew exactly where I was going to wear her: Everett Middle School's Latino Club Dance held every Friday night at St. Peter's Rectory.

I knew that with my new Pendleton I had my chance to enter the pantheon of Mission District cholas. I didn't really want to be a choLA; I wanted to be a choLO. I wasn't sure what that meant, but it was how I felt. All I knew was with that Pendleton, I wouldn't exist near the outer edge of Nerdlandia anymore. Unlike Ray who had a ton of Pendletons and friends who let him drive their lowriders across the Bay Bridge to visit us. And Marlene who with her best friend Mercedes of M&M fame whose names—followed by a C/S—were found on every wall, bench, bus stop, sidewalk in all parts of La Mission—knew guys and girls with cars, guys and girls with lowriders, guys and girls who dropped her off and picked her up blasting "Oh My Angel," "Tell Him," or another cool Oldie. I knew MUNI bus routes.

After my red socks disaster, my sister and Mom taught me about matching clothes: "You can wear a shirt with one color if the pants have that color too. Or vice versa. Simple. Like Garanimals." Back then, I was too old for Garanimals, but I had always been too big.

"Chubby" or "husky," Mom whispered quickly each time she used to take us clothes shopping and I had to buy pants in the boys' department—not that I minded—or with an X after the number: 6X, 8X, 10X,...

"Fat," Marlene reminded me loud and clear even when we weren't in a dressing room.

That morning, I had chosen my Navy BLUE Ben's to match my baby BLUE Pendleton. My outfit was jammin'!

Walking to Everett, I peeked in store windows to catch my shoulders, back, and arms floating inside my Pendleton. As I walked up the steps and beneath the arches and between the giant pillars of the school, I knew this was going to be the best day of my life.

My best friend Gloria joined the rest of our classmates in admiring my Pendleton.

"Ooooh!"

I smiled and tried to be humble.

"That shirt is live!"

I smiled and tried to be humble.

"Where'd *you* get that?"

I smiled then kept walking to first period English.

All day long in my classes, during passing periods, and at lunch, everyone complimented me on my Pendleton, asked where I got it and if they could borrow it. All day long I answered, "Thank you. My brother. No."

After school, me and my Pendleton walked down Mission Street. Me and my Pendleton stopped at the American Music Store to see what new jams were in. Me and my Pendleton looked for a matching flower at Si Tashjian's Flowers and Gifts. Me and my Pendleton lingered in front of Doré Studio's dazzling portraits. Me and my Pendleton bought a strawberry paleta at Latin Freeze. I was very careful not to slurp too hard and spill a single drop. When I came out, the real cholas and cholos stopped and stared at me. Then they kicked up their chins and said, "Welcome to the Cool Club, vata!" Maybe they didn't say it out loud, but I could tell that's what they were thinking from behind their Cleopatra-lined eyes and wraparound 54s. Then me and my Pendleton walked down 24th Street to meet Gloria at Paco's Tacos on South Van Ness. She had stayed after school to finish a homework assignment. We ordered sodas then walked down the last few blocks of 24th before turning right into St. Peter's gate. But the rectory doors were still closed. "Damn!" me and Gloria said at the same time.

Mrs. Novarro and Mr. Ramirez, the club sponsors, were late. The debut of the new me was postponed. Me and my Pendleton and Gloria stood and waited.

That's when SHE, Laura Luz Lavanderos, appeared. Her roasted coffee bean eyes against her toasted almond skin, glimmering white teeth behind wide, pomegranate lips made her the prettiest chola, no, the prettiest girl in *all* of Everett Middle School. Truth is, she was finer than any chola at Mission High too.

My heart would've leaped out of my baby breast-chest if it hadn't been for my Pendleton. And the fact that Laura Luz Lavanderos would've kicked my ass. Laura Luz Lavanderos was co-founder of Las Divinas, Everett's one and only official chola gang. Laura Luz Lavanderos hadn't invited me to be in it. She invited Gloria and Gloria—loyal at all times except for this one—accepted. I was bummed. How insulting not to be invited to join a gang! It turned out to be ok cuz when I fell in love with another girl, I betrayed Gloria. It was a different kind of love, but I didn't know how to tell her, Mom, or anybody. Not even myself. But that's another story for another time.

So, more than wanting to join Laura Luz Lavanderos' gang, I wanted our hearts to join. But she was already in love with Romeo, and he was the fool that kept breaking up with her. All the girls thought he was one of the cutest boys in the neighborhood. Yeah, he sauntered down the street with a bad-boy smile that made you wonder if he had just smoked up or told off a teacher. And he had probably done both. But he wasn't always cute. Or cool. I slept over Gloria's house every Friday night and he lived next door. I heard his mama send him to the store for a carton of milk and yell at him to stop hanging out with his no-good friends. She even slapped his hair out of place once. He wasn't all that. Except to Laura Luz Lavanderos.

"Hi," she said while I stood on the steps of the rectory. I was almost Romeo's height like that.

"Hi, Laura Luz Lavanderos."

"That Pendleton is—why'd you say my whole name?"

"Hi, Laura."

"That Pendleton is firme."

"Thanks...Laura," she looked at me like I was weird.

"Where'd you buy it?"

"My brother gave it to me," I said quickly then forced my lips to stay closed so I wouldn't say any of her names.

"Can I borrow it?"

My Pendleton? I loved Laura Luz Lavanderos, but this was my Pendleton! Laura Luz Lavanderos sensed my doubt, my dread, my fear.

"I'll give it back."

What if she didn't?

"I promise."

What if she was lying?

"You can kick my ass if I don't."

We both knew that wasn't going to happen.

"Your sister can kick my ass if I don't...But I am."

Besides wondering if she would bring back my Pendleton, I couldn't help wondering: if I let her wear my Pendleton, maybe... just maybe...Laura Luz Lavanderos would...see I loved her...then she might discover that deep, deep, very deep inside her heart...she loved me too. Or could love me. Or could like me in that special way.

I unbuttoned my Pendleton and slipped it off. I handed it to Laura Luz Lavanderos. I tried to help her put it on then she looked at me like I was weird again. I knew she was the finest chola between two schools, but with my Pendleton on...she truly was the finest chola in ALL of San Pancho. What propelled her from Mission beauty to All-City?

Black. Laura Luz Lavanderos wore BLACK Ben's. The black Ben's contrasted with the baby blue Pendleton in a way that I could've never imagined. Laura Luz Lavanderos showed me that sure, baby blue can be worn with blue. But the BLACK Ben's made the baby BLUE in the Pendleton flash! And the baby BLUE made Laura Luz Lavanderos' BLACK Ben's look like Mission Street at midnight, familiar but still exciting because you didn't know what would happen. My sister let me hang out with her and her friends one time and we didn't come home until one in the morning! Everything—Sir Jacs, Derbys, Dickies, Lowriders Do It Low and Slow t-shirts— and even my Pendleton looked better on Laura Luz Lavanderos. And she knew it. As Laura Luz Lavanderos strutted away in my Pendleton and her BLACK Ben's, I realized that she had visualized our stunning outfit before she even put on my Pendleton.

Gloria pushed me into the dance. Mrs. Novarro and Mr. Rodriguez had arrived and the dj had set up his gear on a couple of folding tables. The records were playing and the strobe lights were blinking. Gloria sat by me except when she was doing The Worm or The Dog with Sir Weasel or Little Eddie. I moped in the corner. Though when Funkadelic's "One Nation Under a Groove" came on, I couldn't help but lip synch some of the words:

Do you promise to funk
the whole funk
and nothing but the funk?

or

Here's my chance
to dance my way
out of my constriction

I didn't know what constriction meant, but that word clicked in my
ears in a way that I could feel in my soul. I knew my heart was in
constriction.

Two hours later, Laura Luz Lavanderos came back with Romeo.
She found me in my corner and kept her promise. She tossed my
wrinkled Pendleton at me like we meant nothing to her. Then she
slow-danced with Romeo. Then she made out with him right there
on the dance floor. Then she grinded on him. Then she ground on
him. I turned away. Ok, Gloria told me to stop staring.

"Hey, loca! Quit it! She's going to kick your ass if you keep checking
out her man!"

I didn't correct Gloria. How could I? What was I going to say?
"I wasn't checking out Romeo. I was checking out Laura Luz
Lavanderos"? Yeah, right.

I loved Laura Luz Lavanderos. At least I liked her. Very much. And
I knew I wasn't supposed to. No one in my family told me, "Don't
like girls." I just knew I couldn't. Or shouldn't. But I wanted to be
close to Laura Luz Lavanderos...I wanted to get closer and closer...
then kiss her. I hoped it would happen soon. I wasn't confused
about that. While I stared at her, sometimes, I looked at Romeo.
He had muscles, dimples, and his hair combed back nice and
smooth. I didn't want to admit he was a fox cuz he was going with

the girl I wanted to go with. But sometimes I imagined being near him and getting closer and closer and closer...then jumping into his body. Not on top of his body, not next to it but *into* it. Then kissing Laura Luz Lavanderos. It would be him—but really me—finally kissing her. All of that was clear to me. And confused me.

"Let's walk to the phone booth so you can call your Mom and tell her you're sleeping over," Gloria told me when the dj started packing up his milk crates.

"I just remembered that she said she wants me home tonight," I lied. I didn't feel like talking or watching TV or playing games or records all night. Not that night, the worst night of my life.

"You always sleep over on Fridays."

"I know, but we're going to see my Grandpa at Laguna Honda tomorrow. Early."

"All right. I'll walk you to Mission Street."

"Naw, that's ok."

"What?"

"I'll just walk with my sister and her friends."

"WHAT?"

"I'll be fine."

"Are you sure? They'll walk ahead of you and ignore you."

Gloria was there that time Marlene let us hang with her homegirls. One of our friends' little brothers who worked in a liquor store had snuck out a couple pints of Seagram's. I tried to show how cool I was and drank up. First I thought I was sounding big and bad in my mutilated Chola Spanish. Gloria later told me I was yelling and no one could understand me. Then I vomited all over La Squeaky's new jellies. Marlene had to bring me home early that night. Good thing Mom was already in bed when we came in.

"I don't care. I hope they do."

"Are you mad cuz Laura wrinkled your Pendleton?"

"No, I'm just not feeling good."

"Well, don't get your Grandpa sick. Your Nana'll kill you. I'll call you tomorrow."

"Ok."

I caught up to my sister and her friends and walked behind them.

"What's wrong with you?" she asked me when it was just us and we were almost home.

"Nothing."

"If Mom sees you like that she's gonna think I did something."

"You didn't."

"I know. When we get home, you better look happy like you always do."

I tried, but Mom could tell something was wrong with me and looked at my sister. My sister looked at me from behind Mom.

"I got a stomachache." Mom put her hand on my forehead.

"You're a little warm too."

"Yeah, Mom, she's sick. She was weirdly quiet on the way home."

"Go to bed, mija."

"Ok," usually I argued to stay up as late as possible.

"You must be sick. Good night, mija."

"Night, Mom."

I went to my side of the bedroom and very quietly brought out my portable record player and set it on the floor. I chose a 45 from my stash in the closet and found a disk holder. I put it on the spinning wheel and turned the volume to its lowest setting so only I could hear it. Then I laid down. As James and Bobby Purify sang

Pull them little strings
and I'll kiss your lips
I'm your puppet
Snap your fingers
and I'll turn you some flips
I'm your puppet

I rolled around on my bed and cried into my Pendleton over and over and over until I fell asleep.

The next morning, I woke up when Mom came in saying Gloria was on the phone. The record player was off and put away along with the 45.

"She wants to know if you want to go down Mission."

"Yeah! Can I?"

"Yes, if you take a shower and clean up your room. You can thank your sister for putting away your record player last night. I'll tell Gloria you'll call her back in a few minutes."

"Thanks, Mom. I'll thank Marlene too."

"You better hurry. Just wash the important parts."

I started to get out of bed then closed my eyes and fell back. It hit me: I was never going to be good at fashion or get invited to join Las Divinas. Laura Luz Lavanderos didn't love me, didn't like me in that special way, and could barely stand me. And I wasn't jumping into Romeo's body this lifetime.

Then I remembered: I still had my best friend Gloria, my own pair of black Ben's, and the coolest Pendleton. I found it hanging in the closet, grabbed some underwear, and ran down the hall to the shower.

I still have that baby blue Pendleton, and I wear it on special occasions. With black Ben's. Cuz some women appreciate baby blue and black, an Oldie, and walking down Mission Street at midnight.

Dede My SisterCousin

I.
dede teaches me to whistle with my fingers
spins the dryer while i swirl inside
gets a stomach ache and disappears
whenever nana tells us girls to do dishes

dede raises her hand first to be the girlfriend
when we play that game
says she is going to knock
uncle davy's cane out from under him
cuz he pulls the blankets off us when we're asleep
throws pillows at our feet when we're awake

II.
dede moves with her father
marries her sweetheart
has her precious daughter
moves back home when she is too sick
to live 3,000 miles away

dede asks me to take her to the 99 cent store
brings her blue handicapped sign
so we get good parking
treats me to red lobster's crab special
on her disability check
and takes an hour to crack the spidery legs

dede calls the van to take her to general hospital
cuz we all have to work
she asks if i can take her teenager
to do something fun
when the girl comes for a visit

Arellano

III.
dede was a teenager
giggling in the dollar store
a few weeks ago
collapses into baby
in bed with steel bars

when i come in
she puckers her lips hello
she not lover
not mother
but cousin who is sister
i kiss her

"i'm never embarrassed"
she says
"you're my best friend"

her daughter returns
dede's skin warms
her eyes open

the babies run
around the waiting room
down the halls
just outside the ICU door

then saturday night
40-year old dede bawls
"god take me!"

we know what to do
her mother, father, brother, sisters,
our aunts, uncles, cousins
line up two by two
like when we were kids
and wanted a drink of pepsi

when it's my turn
i recognize the familiar shadow
i brush aside plastic band
massage her hand

"if you can hear me
please please please"

she is less than warm
eyes glazed shut
tube-pocked skin connected to
too many boxes and wires

her fingers
squeeze mine
i'm so happy
i don't notice
when she lets go

Gentrification Is When

my land has more value
when you own it

you're invited to the neighborhood association
i've never seen the welcome mat

you move to my neighborhood for diversity
don't do a damn thing to diversify your own hometown

you stroll carefree through my neighborhood
i'm arrested while driving through yours

you buy your house
evict me from my dream home

you move in and Bi-Rite stops stocking
my Nana's #1 ingredient: affordable

bike lanes go up where there always were bikes
just brown riders

hundreds of you are never a mob
two of us is always a gang

the city installs new lights at Dolores Park for you
builds a new jail at 17th and Valencia for me

you think this poem is a joke
i don't care what you think

but i have to

Los Ocho

Sammy leaves his brother Sonny's apartment across from Mission Playground. He heads to the grocery store on the corner to buy cigarettes. He lights his last one when he hears a tank behind him and starts to run. Sonny hears the noise and looks out his window.

"FREEZE!"

Doors crash open as four vehicles grind onto the sidewalk. Six black-clad SWAT members tackle Sammy to the sidewalk. On the way down, they punch and kick him into submission. One from the group yanks Sammy's wallet from his back pocket and tosses it to the lieutenant standing to the side. Then the lieutenant's right hand man joins the circle of fourteen other marksmen encircling Sammy.

Ready.
Aim.
Lock.

"Martinez," the lieutenant calls for Sammy's attention.

Sammy doesn't respond.

"MARTINEZ!"

"Yes," Sammy answers weakly.

"Where are they!"

"Who?"

"Don't fuck with me! Where are your friends!"

"Who? Which--?"

"The ones who killed that cop yesterday"

"I don't know who—"

"Your goddamned hoodlum friends who killed Officer Brodkin yesterday! Where are they?"

"I don't know what-" Sammy starts to answer then he remembers last night's news and this morning's *Chronicle*, "seven Latin hippie types wanted for the murder of an undercover officer..."

"Where were you yesterday!"

Hazy memories clog Sammy's mind.

"Where. Were. You, you f-"

"I'm moving slow. Got my arms up. That's my brother," Sonny enters the circle with his hands behind his head. "He didn't do nothin'. I'm taking him home."

Eyes widen then narrow. Rifles on the left side focus on Sammy. Rifles on the right side now follow Sonny.

"What the hell? Who are you?" asks the lieutenant.

"I'm his brother. I live right there," Sonny points to his window. "We were just having a few drinks when he left for some smokes."

"Martinez fits the description, lieutenant!" the second-in-charge reminds the officer.

"We're moving slow," Sonny reaches for Sammy. "We got our arms up," he nudges Sammy's arms.

Sammy weakly raises his arms and starts to climb to a kneeling position.

"We ain't got nothing on us. We're clean," Sonny repeats.

"We need to take him in for questioning," the lieutenant presses Sammy's shoulder until he's flat on the ground again.

"He's Navy. Just back from 'Nam. Settling in again," Sonny tells the lieutenant.

"You sure he wasn't hiding up in Canada. Or Mexico?" the lieutenant asks then spits.

"He was on a gunboat. I was in Korea. Air Defense Artillery. It takes a while to come home after you ain't been home," Sonny pulls Sammy to his knees.

"You guys know how it is." Sonny looks at the lieutenant then the rest of his team. Some look away. The lieutenant grips Sammy's shoulder. All fingers stay on all triggers.

"He's so fucken shit-happy to be home," Sonny says eyeing the lieutenant's hand, laughing before catching himself. "He has a few drinks now and then," Sonny says looking directly at the lieutenant. "But he doesn't bring trouble to my mother cuz he knows I'll kick his ass."

Sonny lifts Sammy to a standing position. The lieutenant scowls and steps in Sammy's way.

"Whatever happened," Sonny says, "it wasn't him. And he don't know nothing about it."

The lieutenant doesn't move.

"He'll be here all night if you need to come back," Sonny nods toward his apartment. "Number 3. If he's not here, he'll be at my mother's. The address on his license."

Sonny steers Sammy around the lieutenant and toward the brick building he calls home. Sammy stumbles. The lieutenant hesitates then throws Sammy's ID at Sonny's feet.

"Fuck 'Nam and Korea!" The lieutenant spits out.

Sonny turns around.

"I don't give a shit if you two spics wore uniforms. If we come back, I'll take both your asses in for public drunkenness, resisting arrest, and anything else I can think of!"

He waves his men to drop their rifles. Fifteen triggers release. Doors slam. Four wagons jump off the curb.

Sonny steadies Sammy then reaches for his brother's ID. He reaches around Sammy's waist and Sammy puts his arm around Sonny's shoulder. The brothers walk inside the building and Sonny closes the door.

Sonny begs Betty Jean to stay in the bedroom with the baby. After six straight cans of Oly, Sammy passes out on the sofa. Sonny doesn't sleep. He hears his baby girl crying in the bedroom and her mama sh-shing her. He slaps Sammy's head. Sammy only snores louder. When Sonny sees slow-moving headlights approach, he peeks through the slit between the curtain and the window. If—when—they come back, he knows there won't be anything he can do. Except all he can. Sonny closes his eyes and waits.

Dolores Park May 2011

we invoke the parking goddess
and find a spot
in ten minutes max
we carry bags
walk down the slope
above the playground
pull out sandwiches and sodas
sit and feast

in between bites
i point out
      the bell
            where us five sistercousins
            flew past the milky way
            on our way to candy land
            on that smooth slab of concrete base
      mission high across the street
            since 1944
            family herded through one door
            and out the other
            sometimes with a diploma
      thirty-eight oh two
            two bedrooms
            two half bathrooms
            so many mouths to feed
            we ate in shifts

the sweet smell of weed
coming from white girl private party next to us
distracts geen

      the basketball court
      where we played
      and could be watched
      from an open window

Arellano

paletero's bell announces arrival
white girls wave brown man over
they rip open wrappers
cackle when it's time to pay
turn purses inside out
lick sticky fingers
pass sticky coins

brown child walks up
holds dollar, places order
paletero pockets the bill
rummages through his frozen box

sweet smoke doesn't slow

if this park
this neighborhood
were still irish and italian—
the sons of norway
still held their meetings
a few blocks away—
and brown girls
(heaven forbid brown boys)
were kicking back
with a pipe
while a white child
stood a foot away
to buy an ice cream
how long would it take
before the cops were called?

when the first
whiff of smoke
hit the kid?

when the kid
first saw the pipe?

my mind jumps
from neighborhood
to state
to nation

it swims back 235 years
when the ohlone and miwok walked freely
on their land
now their graves
lie beneath this park
i tread the choppy waters
of 500 years

child coughs
women howl
paletero passes sweet ice
child runs away

i resist my urge to make a citizen's arrest
resist my desire to make my case with my fist
i want to come back another day
i want to come home
sit in the warmth
park my protest sign
and nibble on a paleta

we pack our leftovers
and climb the hill

i unlock the car door
can't climb in
can't drive away
i walk back down

Arellano

stand in front of the smirks
swallow my fists

i whittle all my wars
to one battle

"don't smoke in front of the kids"

If You Can't on Mission Street

if no one asks you for money
the time, a date
if no one asks you to buy a
"late night-late night, fast pass, passport"

if the savvy entrepreneur doesn't stop you
when you pass the paperback books
of his crack mart spread on a tarp
between the falafel place and roxie theater

cholitas with cleopatra eyes
don't maddog you
homies parked on 19th or 24th
don't ask, "what you claim?"

the tamale lady doesn't nod to her cooler
when you rise from the BART cave
the flores lady doesn't wave a bouquet
when you're ordering at la taquería

if a kid on a swing at mission playground
doesn't ask you to push "higher! higher!"
a child on the merry-go-round at dolores park
doesn't ask you to "spin it! spin it!"

if the cristianos don't alleluia you
invite you to their storefront for salvation
hand you a free *watchtower*
or *awake* magazine

the paletero doesn't ring his bell
when he passes you
the fruit lady doesn't offer "elote, mango"
when you pass her

if the cd sellers don't let you look through their cases
and blast a sample on their boom boxes
the dvd vendors don't sell yesterday's new release
at today's special price

if a señora doesn't accept your offer of help
with her bolsas of food
or the lady with a baby
doesn't accept your seat on the 14

the young multilingual latina
doesn't stop folding clothes
the asian or palestinian store owners
don't watch you when you walk in

the man with the red-painted face
doesn't smile at you
the woman with baby-powdered eyelashes
doesn't blink at you

the filipino guy who smokes invisible cigarettes
doesn't salute you
as he marches up and down
the coolest street in town

if somebody passes by and doesn't speak to you in english
mexican puertorican cuban or south american spanish
spanglish caló a dialect of mayan quiché quechua
tagalog vietnamese cantonese mandarin sámoan

then
pack up your cameras
but leave the photos
of all the people
you never asked permission
to steal their image

don't bother calling your job
the place that says
they want to help our community
by telling us what we want
or they're improving our community
by kicking us out

go save some truly at-risk people
in an under-served place
your folks
your home

jump on a bus
call a cab
run don't walk
and don't ever
and I mean EVER
come back

adios
con safos
por vida
y
punto final!

Martinez Family Map, 1958-1984

3581 - 19th Street (1958)
Auntie Ellie and Uncle Sal brought Lola from the hospital here above the store kitty corner from Sun Valley. The one across a street and past another store that was too far to go to unless we were on our way to Mission Playground. By the time Freddy and JJ were born, they had already moved down Highway 1 to Pacifica. They had no idea Denise and I would later sneak peeks at the *Playgirl* centerfolds until we giggled too loud and the owner kicked us out.

35 Dearborn (1960)
Auntie Daisy and Uncle Marco moved to this small, quiet street before Nana made it one of her headquarters years later. This was Nancy's first home when she was the only child for a very short time.

797 Valencia (1962)
Nana and Grandpa moved to a flat off 19th after they lost the house in Pacifica and returned to the City. There's a photo of the uncles standing in front of the building left to right: skinny Uncle Auggie smiling innocently before shipping out to Vietnam, Uncle Davy's quick right fist dangles at the bottom of his Pendleton, Uncle Manny's hands rest on his younger brothers' shoulders, Uncle Sonny is wickedly handsome and invites love or trouble in his white t-shirt and black chinos, scrawny Uncle Sammy's glasses blur his eyes even before his exposure to Agent Orange.

3802 – 18th Street (1966)
This is where me, Mom, and Marlene lived with Nana and Grandpa. Uncle Davy, Uncle Auggie, Uncle Sonny, and Dinky. Auntie Daisy, Nancy, Dede, Denise, and Markie. This is where Uncle Sonny never came home again.

575 Castro (1968)
Mom and Dad took us to visit Uncle Sonny and Auntie Betty Jean in the Castro when Harvey Milk was still in New York. We walked up Castro then turned in at the neon sign. Us kids stopped in front of a tray filled with glaze, sugar, and jelly donuts. Mom nudged us to the back door, held my hand as we climbed the wooden steps in the dark. Before we reached the top, Uncle Sonny boomed, "Look who's here!"

3938 – 18th Street (1968)
Auntie Maggie and Uncle Paul lived in that apartment next to Jenny Padua's between Sanchez and Noe. One day the school bus passed by and we all saw what Jenny saw and still told her, "Your house is on fire!"

3579 – 19th Street (1969)
Uncle Sonny and Auntie Betty Jean lived half a block from Mission Playground. When they first moved back to the City, the uncles hung out at its basketball court, played tennis and baseball when they cut classes at Mission High.

3476 – 19th Street (1969)
Around the corner from Nana and Grandpa, this is where Mom and Dad and us four lived together. This is where me and my sister wore the same velvet Christmas dresses, one in in red, the other in green. Where Dad flipped silver dollar pancakes on Sundays. Where the boys and us girls ran around in our chonis before Mom gave us a bath. Where Dad rented a garage around the corner on Lexington.

636 Guerrero (1969)
After Uncle Sonny and Auntie Betty Jean found a new place and moved around the corner, Auntie Maggie and Uncle Paul moved in when Stephie was a baby. Halfway to Sun Valley on the corner is that Samoan church. Simple black and white paint on the outside. All the color was on the girls and women's dresses. Every Sunday looked like Easter Sunday. Someone in my family rented this flat for more than 35 years.

634A Guerrero Street (1971)
After Nana packed away Uncle Sonny's quilt forever, Mom moved us downstairs from Auntie Maggie. Uncle Auggie lived with us until he got married. Then Uncle Manny took over his bedroom and I found his *Playboy* magazines.

630 Guerrero (1972)
Nana moved next door to us. One day her sister Donna visited. She went from Nana's side of the wall to ours holding a large, paper grocery bag. "Special delivery!" She opened the bag and there was Baby Jessie.

191 Landers (1972)

Auntie Daisy moved across from Mission Dolores. The catechism teacher drew a huge bumble bee on the board and said, "If you commit a sin you'll go to hell and bees will sting you over and over forever."

39 Dearborn (1979)

After middle school, we moved with Nana to the alley across the street from that place where we never went to when it was called The Sons of Norway or The Women's Building. Most of us eventually passed through the bar on the corner, The Dovre Club where pregnant Jessie became our family's pool shark.

268 Delong (1982)

Auntie Susana, Nana's sister and rare homeowner in the family, let Nana rent a second house she owned a few doors down from her own after Nana retired from St. Luke's. Renting to Nana meant opening the floodgate to at least one of her kids and their kids on top of daily visits from the rest of us. A few blocks from Daly City BART, a few blocks from that part of Mission Street we only saw when we caught the Sam Trans bus to Top-of-the-Hill DALY City!

636 – 20th Street (1983)

After the new owner evicted us from our second story, sun-filled, hardwood floor flat, Mom took us to her Tía Nancy's place on Third Street in Dogpatch. Took us to where she grew up 40 years earlier. My first morning of classes at State, Mom got out on her side and set up her compacts, bottles, and tubes on the bed. She opened her powder, brushed the packed grains, looked into the mirror, and as she blew away stray granules sighed: "Get up, mija."

2 Edna (1984)

Mom's friend rented her an apartment called a mother-in-law. Mom got sick and Nana convinced a hospital to admit her after another one wouldn't. We didn't know Mom was going to live there. For a month. Didn't know she was going to die there. Didn't know I was going to die there too.

Acknowledgments

With much gratitude:

Amaryllis DeJesus Moleski for allowing me to use her fabulous image for the cover and Rebekah Tarin for helping me find her.

Readers for pointing out bumps and finding beauty in earlier versions of this manuscript: Estela de la Cruz, Lisa Gill, Jennifer Laflam, Vero Majano, Maria Pedrosa.

Lorna Dee for permission to borrow her words and offering a few more.

Karla, Kathy, Levi, Richard, and Norman for helping a writer out.

Met lots of cool folks in New Mexico but these activists, organizers, artists/writers, land lovers, farmers, teachers opened their hearts and helped me make home when I was a thousand miles from the Bay: beva, Jeana, Sofía, Richard, Andrea, Michelle, Henry, Carlos, Mary, Catalina mi tocaya, Adriann, Tannia, Dolores, Micaela, Mireya, Denicia, Juba, Helene, Monie, Jessica, Gigi, Triplet Huong, Triplet and body double Alice.

I believed Reid back when she talked about the power of story. Every day I believe her more.

The Mission High and Cal folks who survived school and Bay Area Community arts/writing groups, trios, and duets over the years Sergio, Augie, Joel, Kristy, Irene, Dolissa,...

For the conversations, performances, and creations Sandra, Darren, Juana Alicia, Jose, Leticia,...

Diane, Jesse, Ricardo for Proyecto ContraSIDA Por Vida (PCPV) and convening an incredible mass of artists, activists, makers, organizers, lovers, rebels, outlaws who still inspire me: Rebeka, Emael, Marcia, Sarah, Wura, Tisa, Jaime, Al, Gigi, Karla, Bertha, Pato, Prado, Mariah, Loras, and of course Horacio.

Indígena as Scribe for your open hearts and critical ears so many moons ago. Special thank you to Martivón for snacks every week, Lisa for keen reading, Odilia for keeping it real.

Ana Baíz, Junko Kobayashi, Maria Lavanderos, Tanya Mayo, Ixchel Rosal for being near even when far.

Cousins Fran, Teddy, Lucha, Joanna, Krissy, Teo, Laura, Phil, Jimmy, Michelle, Antoinette, Tony, Tommy, and Michael who gave childhood and give adulthood a certain *je ne sais quoi*.

Anita Padilla, Isabel Oden, Rita Castro, Robert Lopez, Michael Lopez, Tom Lopez for teaching me to share even when I didn't want to, the talks, the music, the love, especially since 1984.

Tomasa Arellano Torres and Alejandra Arellano Holmes for the history lessons and love.

Lisa, Michael, and Chris for letting me be the little sister when I needed it most. You weren't much older than I was.

Lorenzo Herrera y Lozano for asking then asking again, keeping us on schedule, nudging me away from bad ideas, loving the good ones.

Celia Herrera Rodríguez for the epic, timeless lessons in simplest ways.

Cherríe Moraga who read early drafts and still had faith. Who teaches me so much as maestra, instills new lessons as comadre. I can only hope to one day work as hard, think as deeply, love as fiercely.

Gina Díaz who dances in heels backwards as I struggle to follow, creates beauty wherever we are.

To those who shared/share works of beauty and strength when I was/am stuck in doubt, fear, and insecurity.

Mucho much thanks to everyone listed and everyone whose name is written in invisible ink. All the errors are mine.

About Cathy Arellano

Just another writer from The Mission, Cathy Arellano worked as a community poet with Loco Bloco and Mission Girls; and at the Mission Cultural Center, Everett Middle, and Mission High Schools through the San Francisco Arts Commission's WritersCorps program; Horace Mann Middle School with the Mexican Museum's community arts workshop; and elementary schools in the Richmond District with the California Poets in the Schools literary series. Later, she became a faculty member in the English Departments at John O'Connell and Leadership High Schools.

Arellano's work is published in print and online, including *La Bloga, Chicana Lesbians: The Girls Our Mothers Warned Us About, Cipactli, Curve Magazine, Days I Moved Through Ordinary Sounds, Duke City Fix, El Tecolote, Feminist Formations, Fourteen Hills, Huizache, Label Me Latino, The Malpaís Review, The Más Tequila Review, Sinister Wisdom: A Multicultural Lesbian Literary & Arts Journal, Tongues Magazine, La Voz,* and *Poetry of Resistance: Voices for Social Justice,* which responds to Arizona's SB 1070 law that legalized racial profiling and allowed police to stop people suspected of being in the U.S. without papers.

She has won awards from the San Francisco Art Commission, the Taos Summer Writers' Conference, and Serpent Source Foundation for Women Artists.

Arellano left the Mission and moved to Albuquerque, New Mexico on the Three to Five Year Plan that turned into seven. She found a vibrant and supportive group of folks that helped resurrect her writing life. Arellano believes deeply in the power of art and community and is grateful to the artists and activists she has created and marched with and been inspired by in the Mission, the Bay, Búrque, and beyond.

OTHER KÓRIMA PRESS TITLES